The Best of Casual Country Cooking

COUNTRY INN

SUNSET BOOKS INC.
Chief Executive Officer: Stephen J. Seabolt
President and Publisher: Susan J. Maruyama
VP, Chief Financial Officer: James E. Mitchell
VP, Manufacturing Director: Lorinda Reichert
Director, Sales and Marketing: Richard A. Smeby
Editorial Director: Bob Doyle
Director of Finance: Lawrence J. Diamond
Production Director: Lory Day
Retail Sales Development Manager: Becky Ellis
Art Director: Vasken Guiragossian

Produced by
WELDON OWEN INC.
President: John Owen
Publisher/Vice President: Wendely Harvey
Chief Financial Officer: Larry Partington
Managing Editor: Lisa Chaney Atwood
Project Coordinator: Jill Fox
Consulting Editor: Norman Kolpas
Copy Editor: Sharon Silva
Designer: Patty Hill
Production Director: Stephanie Sherman
Production Manager: Jen Dalton
Production Editor: Sarah Lemas
Co-Editions Director: Derek Barton
Food Photography: Penina
Food Stylist: Pouké
Assistant Food Stylist: Michelle Syracuse
Prop Stylist: Sara Slavin
Half-Title Illustration: Martha Anne Booth
Chapter Opener Illustrations: Anita Lovitt
Glossary Illustrations: Alice Harth
Photo Research: Amelia Ames Hill

Production by Kyodo Printing Co.
(S'pore) Pte Ltd
Printed in Singapore

First Printing 1997
10 9 8 7 6 5 4 3 2 1

ISBN 0-376-02042-3
Library of Congress Catalog Card Number: 97-3606

A Note on Weights and Measures:
All recipes include customary U.S. and metric measurements.
Metric conversions are based on a standard developed for these
books and have been rounded off. Actual weights may vary.

The Best of Casual Country Cooking

COUNTRY INN

by George Mahaffey

Contents

Afternoon Tea 61

Dinner 83

Dessert 107

Introduction

Yꙮou are motoring along a serene country road bordered by verdant meadows or across a hauntingly dramatic desert mesa or through a chain of mountain peaks. Your drive may hold a number of stops, but at day's end you wish for only one thing: a gracious reception and a comforting meal in a beautiful setting.

That destination is the American country inn, a welcome retreat from the hectic pace of modern life. Often housed in structures of architectural or historical significance—an old mill, a onetime roadhouse, a rural manor, a rambling farmhouse or a former tavern—the country inn is renowned for a style that marries good food with a casual ambience for travelers and locals alike.

A kitchen at one of these establishments prepares dishes that are evocative of the region, pairing the classic with the contemporary and using what is seasonal and local. Menus range from hearty breakfasts to satisfying lunches to comforting afternoon tea to rustic yet stylish dinners to delicious desserts. Such fare makes the country inn the ideal spot to unwind and enjoy memorable meals in a relaxed environment. This book will help you re-create your own country inn dining memories at home.

The History of the Country Inn

In ancient times, inns flourished along travel and trade routes. In Persia, large fortresslike structures called caravansaries offered rudimentary lodging to sojourners, but no food. During Roman times, inns prospered in cities as well. In the Middle Ages, accommodations for travelers became limited primarily to what was available in monasteries. The Renaissance brought the revitalization of commerce and the rising popularity of religious pilgrimages, so that privately run lodging houses began to spring up once again. By the end of the 16th century, inns in Great Britain alone numbered over five thousand and routinely offered simple meals to their guests.

Colonial America saw the tavern become a center of community activity, providing a meeting place for locals and lodging for travelers. Rudimentary sleeping quarters with only a frame bed, a nightstand, and a ceramic basin were the standard. Nevertheless, this forerunner of the contemporary country inn was a place to obtain hearty meals of dependable, if not noteworthy, quality.

Two centuries later, the opening up of the American West saw the establishment of roadhouses and way stations along the well-traveled routes.

With the railroads came railroad hotels and the concept of the inn not only as a necessary traveler's amenity, but also as a vacationer's retreat. This new role brought a greater emphasis on the quality of an inn's food. Handsome parlors that mimicked the grand dining salons of city hotels and menus featuring daily specials and regional favorites became the norm, and the idea of taking tea in the afternoon with light snacks became a fashion that is still enjoyed today.

Perhaps nowhere else has country inn hospitality become so embedded as it has in America during the past 30 years. It is inspired by the understated elegance of the French auberge, as well as the tradition of service and charm of the English country house.

From America's rich heritage of innkeeping has come a distinctive new cuisine, casual yet elegant American country cooking built upon regional influences and seasonally available local ingredients. No longer

just popular meeting places or stopovers, country inns today have become inviting resort destinations prized for the quality of their food and their casual ambience.

The Inn Experience

Picture yourself at a country inn for the day. Breakfast could well be a bountiful buffet of cereals, home-baked breads and pastries, fruits, juices, yogurt and coffee. Other times you might select your meal from a menu that includes eggs or a stack of feather-light pancakes. At lunchtime, take advantage of the sun-warmed terrace to enjoy soups, salads and sandwiches made from local ingredients. Or if sightseeing or a hike is on the agenda, tote along a portable feast.

During a long, lazy afternoon, unwind over a pot of tea or a pitcher of lemonade and a few small sandwiches, a freshly baked scone, a tartlet or tea cookies. When evening arrives, make your way to the dining room, where the menu offers a diverse

range of selections, from grilled fish and chicken to such classics as braised beef, rack of pork and leg of lamb. The chef might even prepare a sampler platter of smaller portions. Cap off your day with a selection from a tempting list of desserts.

The inn's decor will reflect its region, from the easy charm of an 18th-century New England farmhouse or a modern, firelit ski chalet to a Southwest inn constructed of adobe and decorated with stunning cacti. Tastes of Europe—an Italian villa, a French auberge, an English country home—are woven into the fabric of the modern American country inn, too, in decor, cuisine and traditions of hospitality.

The Country Inn at Home

The hallmark of country inn cuisine is its simplicity and its reliance on fresh, seasonal foods. Fortunately, modern shipping makes it possible for the home cook to obtain practically any product needed to echo a meal enjoyed at even the most distant inn.

To recapture the same rustic warmth in your home, scout local flea markets, crafts fairs and garage sales for distinctive table decor and serving pieces. Remember that not every detail needs to be unique or expensive. Any homey pieces will work well. Decorate with fresh-cut flowers and you have set the stage for your own truly unforgettable country inn experience.

Beverages

A visit to any contemporary inn reveals a wealth of beverage offerings. From the coffee gourmet to the enologist, from the tea lover to the aficionado of micro-brewed beers, from the fitness buff to the child looking for a glass of ice-cold milk, the appropriate beverage is always within reach.

Breakfast

Breakfast usually features a variety of fresh-squeezed fruit juices such as orange and grapefruit, and vegetable juices from carrot to tomato to a variety of intriguing blends.

Coffee, of course, remains the beverage mainstay of the morning meal, and much attention is paid to its preparation by the innkeeper.

Guests who crave something sweet at the start of the day will often find hot cocoa offered as well. Ideally, it is served while still frothy, topped with softly whipped cream and a dash of ground cinnamon.

Lunch

A country inn at midday prompts the offering of a tremendous variety of beverages. Whether guests are enjoying a noontime work break, a full lunch, or a light repast in anticipation of an afternoon hike, they will find a drink to suit the circumstances. In warm weather, there is iced coffee, seltzer transformed into a host of refreshing variations by infusing it with fruit juices, or a cooling, healthful *agua fresca* (see recipe at right). In winter-time, the noon hour finds guests clutching mugs of hot cider or full-bodied vegetable broth.

Afternoon Tea

Although afternoon tea is a daily event at many contemporary country inns, its form varies widely, so that the traditional pot of tea is commonly joined by everything from cocktails to hot chocolate. On a hot summer's day at a western guest ranch, afternoon tea taken in the shade of a spreading tree includes iced tea, beer, lemonade and mineral water. On a chilly winter's day at a mountain ski resort, a crackling fire calls for pots of steaming tea, plus hot cider or hot cocoa. Whether you call it high tea or happy hour, afternoon beverage service accompanied with sweet and savory snacks is a hallmark of the country inn, a chance for guests to mingle and relax from the rigors of vacation. At home, make simple plans for tea or cocktail enter-taining, which will leave you free to relax and enjoy a brief holiday with friends and family.

Dinner

The most popular accompaniment to a country inn dinner is wine. A bottle of mineral water is also com-monly poured, and for the sake of any children or nondrinkers, fruit juice, soft drinks and iced tea are also offered. In general, serve a white wine with lighter-bodied foods, first courses, seafood, poultry, pork and veal. When spiciness, sweetness, and smoky flavors imparted by grilling are factors, however, certain red wines work well, too. The progression of courses defines what wine is served as well. If the first course is a light salad or soup followed by, for example, short ribs, a crisp white wine should launch the meal, to be followed by a full-bodied red. Do not be afraid to make your own judgment about which wine to drink, breaking traditional rules in favor of personal taste.

For serving wines in your home, a decent corkscrew and glasses appropriate to the wines being served are more crucial than expensive decanters or other related paraphernalia. White wines should be chilled, while reds are best enjoyed at slightly warmer than refrigerated levels.

When all is said and done, however, the first rule of wine service is not to run out. With this caveat in mind, plan on six ounces per person of each wine being poured.

Dessert

Espresso and other coffee drinks are popularly served along with dessert in a country inn, rather than following it. Guests will also likely sample from an array of dessert wine selections. Lighter, less sweet or sparkling wines are generally best with richer desserts, port complements chocolates, and sweeter wines pair well with fruits. Cognac, Armagnac and Calvados, all of which are said to settle the stomach, are often served at the end of the meal.

AGUA FRESCA

This thirst-quenching beverage, Spanish for "fresh water," is a wonderful addition to any informal country inn menu.

2   cups (12 oz/375 g) peeled, seeded and diced ripe fruit such as melon, pineapple, mango and/or papaya
2½   cups (20 fl oz/625 ml) water, preferably filtered
3   tablespoons sugar

♔ In a blender or a food processor fitted with the metal blade, combine the fruit, water and sugar. Process on high speed until completely smooth, about 1 minute.

♔ Pass through a fine-mesh sieve, pressing with the back of a spoon to extract as much juice as possible. Chill thoroughly before serving.

Serves 4

Basic Recipes

Country inn cuisine derives from a vast range of sources. Despite this wide variety, some of the cooking basics are constant, including a stock, a simple pastry cream and easy pie doughs.

SAVORY PASTRY DOUGH

The less this dough is worked, the more flaky the final pastry will be.

2½ cups (12½ oz/390 g) all-purpose (plain) flour
½   teaspoon salt
15 tablespoons (7½ oz/235 g) chilled unsalted butter, cut into pieces
5   tablespoons (3 fl oz/ 80 ml) ice water

⚜ In a bowl, stir together the flour and salt. Add the butter pieces and, using a pastry blender or a fork, cut in the butter until the mixture looks crumbly and the butter is in pea-sized pieces. Add the ice water and, using a wooden spoon, work in very briefly to form a rough dough. Do not make the dough a smooth, homogeneous ball. Work unincorporated flour into the dough when rolling out.

⚜ Wrap the dough and loose flour particles in plastic wrap and refrigerate for at least 1 hour or for up to 1 week before use.

Makes two 9-inch (23-cm) pie shells

SWEET PASTRY DOUGH

The addition of sugar and egg makes this the richer cousin of a standard pie pastry dough. It bakes to a crisp, more cookielike texture than the savory pastry and is perfect for the lemon galette on page 116.

1½ cups (7½ oz/235 g) all-purpose (plain) flour
5   tablespoons (2½ oz/75 g) sugar
⅛   teaspoon salt
10 tablespoons (5 oz/155 g) unsalted butter, at room temperature
1   whole egg, plus 2 egg yolks

⚜ In a bowl, combine the flour, sugar, salt and butter. Using a heavy-duty stand mixer fitted with the paddle attachment or a handheld electric mixer, beat on medium speed until the butter is well coated with the flour and is broken into small pieces. Add the egg and egg yolks and beat together until the mixture comes together in a smooth dough.

⚜ Remove from the bowl, gather into a ball, wrap in plastic wrap and refrigerate for at least 1 hour or for up to 1 week before use.

Makes one 10-inch (25-cm) tart shell or four 4-inch (10-cm) tart shells or 1 galette shell

PASTRY CREAM

Pastry cream is a classic of the dessert world. It is used as a filling or topping for tarts, éclairs and cream puffs, and is called for in a number of the desserts beginning on page 108.

2¼ cups (18 fl oz/560 ml) milk
½ cup (4 fl oz/125 ml) heavy (double) cream
¾ cup (6 oz/185 g) sugar
5 tablespoons (1½ oz/45 g) cornstarch (cornflour)
1 whole egg, plus 1 egg yolk
1 teaspoon vanilla extract (essence)

✢ In a heavy saucepan over medium heat, combine 1½ cups (12 fl oz/ 375 ml) of the milk, the cream and sugar and bring almost to a boil, whisking once or twice to dissolve the sugar. While this mixture is heating, place the cornstarch in a small bowl and add ½ cup (4 fl oz/125 ml) of the milk, stirring to dissolve the cornstarch. Add the remaining ¼ cup (2 fl oz/60 ml) milk, the whole egg, egg yolk and vanilla. Whisk together until smooth.

✢ When the hot milk mixture is about to boil, pour in the cornstarch mixture, whisking continuously until completely blended. Continue to heat the mixture, whisking constantly, until it boils and thickens to the consistency of custard pudding. Remove from the heat, pour into a bowl and press a piece of plastic wrap directly onto the surface to prevent a skin from forming. Let cool completely before using or refrigerating. Refrigerate for up to 1 week before use.

Makes 3 cups (24 fl oz/750 ml)

CHICKEN STOCK

This kitchen staple can be prepared ahead and frozen for up to a month. Homemade stock is a wonderful use of either inexpensive chicken bones or the carcass and remains from a roasted chicken. By making it yourself, you can flavor it to your own taste. If you need to substitute canned broth or stock, look for low-sodium versions and add your favorite spices and herbs.

2½ qt (2.5 l) water
1 lb (500 g) chicken bones or carcass of roasted 3½-lb (1.75-kg) chicken
1 yellow onion, cut up
1 celery stalk, cut up
1 carrot, peeled and cut up
2 fresh flat-leaf (Italian) parsley sprigs
½ teaspoon salt
½ teaspoon dried thyme
¼ teaspoon peppercorns
1 bay leaf

✢ In a stock pot over medium-high heat, combine the water and chicken and bring slowly to a boil. Skim off any scum that rises to the surface. Add the onion, celery, carrot, parsley, salt, thyme, peppercorns and bay leaf. Reduce the heat to medium and simmer, uncovered, for 2 hours. Check from time to time and skim off scum that appears on the surface.

✢ Remove from the heat and let cool for 15 minutes. Strain through a fine-mesh sieve into a large bowl and use immediately. Or let cool, cover and refrigerate for up to 5 days or freeze for up to 1 month before use. Before using, remove and discard any fat congealed on top.

Makes about 6 cups (48 fl oz/1.5 l)

Breakfast

ornings in the dining room of a country inn can be a hurried affair or a time to relax. For those anxious to start the day, there is usually a buffet featuring cereals and sliced fresh fruits, homemade muffins and piping-hot beignets, yogurt and just-squeezed juices. Guests in search of a more leisurely breakfast can peruse the menu and choose between delicious specialties from eggs Benedict made with corn bread and Virginia ham to thickly cut French toast drizzled with warm maple syrup. Fresh coffee, often brewed from a blend custom-designed for the inn, is poured into handsome china cups or ceramic mugs, and refreshed throughout the meal.

To create your own country inn breakfast, set a simple table and dress it up with brightly colored napkins and an attractive bud vase or two holding fresh-cut flowers. Put out as many of the traditional morning condiments—jams, jellies, preserves, whipped butter, milk or cream, honey, syrups—as you can assemble. Thoughtful presentation touches—small ceramic bowls in place of traditional jam caddies, a decorative glass pitcher for fresh juice, containers of seasonal fruit, a pot of freshly ground and brewed coffee—will recall breakfast service at your favorite inn.

Granola with Yogurt

Three types of nuts give this granola a satisfying texture and a pleasant richness. The slow roasting of the ingredients heightens their flavors and extends the shelf life of the cereal. The granola can be stored in a tightly sealed container at room temperature for 2 weeks.

2 cups (6 oz/185 g) old-fashioned rolled oats

¾ cup (2½ oz/75 g) wheat germ

¼ cup (1½ oz/45 g) macadamia nuts, coarsely chopped

¼ cup (1 oz/30 g) walnuts, coarsely chopped

¼ cup (1 oz/30 g) blanched sliced (flaked) almonds

¼ cup (1½ oz/45 g) shelled sunflower seeds

6 tablespoons (5 oz/155 g) honey

½ cup (4 fl oz/125 ml) canola oil

¼ teaspoon vanilla extract (essence)

1½ teaspoons ground cinnamon

¼ teaspoon ground nutmeg

2 cups (16 oz/500 g) plain yogurt

1 cup (4 oz/125 g) mixed berries such as raspberries, strawberries and blueberries, stems removed if necessary

4 fresh mint sprigs

🥄 Preheat an oven to 225°F (105°C).

🥄 In a large bowl, stir together the oats, wheat germ, macadamia nuts, walnuts, almonds and sunflower seeds. In a small saucepan over low heat, combine the honey and the oil and heat until the honey liquefies. Add the vanilla, cinnamon and nutmeg and stir well. Let cool for 1 minute.

🥄 Drizzle the honey mixture over the oat mixture and, using your hands, rub together until all of the ingredients are thoroughly coated. Turn out the mixture onto a baking sheet and spread it evenly.

🥄 Bake until a deep golden brown, about 2½ hours, stirring once at the halfway point to ensure even coloring. Remove from the oven and let cool completely.

🥄 To serve, divide evenly among cereal bowls. While holding the granola to one side, spoon an equal amount of the yogurt into the open half of each bowl. Garnish with the berries and mint sprigs.

Serves 4

Lemon Soufflé Pancakes with Raspberry Syrup

*The dulcet texture and flavor of these light pancakes are complemented
superbly by the fruitiness of the raspberry syrup, although commercial fruit syrup or
preserves can provide an equally enjoyable and simpler-to-prepare topping.*

1   cup (5 oz/155 g) plus 2 tablespoons all-purpose (plain) flour
3   tablespoons granulated sugar
1½ teaspoons baking powder
½   teaspoon salt
¼   teaspoon ground nutmeg
    Grated zest of 5 lemons
¾   cup (6 oz/185 g) ricotta cheese
6   tablespoons (3 fl oz/90 ml) buttermilk
6   tablespoons (3 oz/90 g) unsalted butter, melted and kept warm
2   tablespoons fresh lemon juice
¾   teaspoon vanilla extract (essence)
3   eggs, separated

RASPBERRY SYRUP
1½ cups (12 fl oz/375 ml) corn syrup
1½ cups (6 oz/185 g) raspberries
1½ tablespoons fresh lemon juice

    Nonstick cooking spray
    Confectioners' (icing) sugar
    Fresh mint sprigs

⚜ In a large bowl, stir together the flour, 1 tablespoon of the granulated sugar, the baking powder, salt, nutmeg and lemon zest.

⚜ In a small bowl, combine the ricotta cheese, buttermilk, melted butter, lemon juice, vanilla extract and egg yolks and whisk until smooth. Add the yolk mixture to the flour mixture and whisk together until smooth. The batter will be quite dense.

⚜ In a bowl, using a mixer set on medium speed, beat the egg whites until soft peaks form. Sprinkle in the remaining 2 tablespoons sugar and continue beating until stiff peaks form. Using a rubber spatula, carefully fold about one-fourth of the egg whites into the batter, then fold in the remaining egg whites. Do not attempt to make the batter completely uniform; a few streaks of egg white are fine. Cover and refrigerate for up to 1 hour.

⚜ To make the raspberry syrup, in a small saucepan over medium heat, combine the corn syrup, raspberries and lemon juice. Bring slowly to a boil. Reduce the heat to low and continue to cook at a bare simmer until a light, crimson-colored syrup forms, about 20 minutes. Remove from the heat and immediately strain through a fine-mesh sieve into a bowl, pressing on the berry pulp with the back of a spoon to extract as much liquid as possible. Cover to keep warm.

⚜ Lightly coat a griddle or a large nonstick frying pan with nonstick cooking spray, then preheat over medium heat for 2–3 minutes. For each pancake, spoon about ¾ cup (6 fl oz/180 ml) of the batter into the pan, to form rough cakes about 5 inches (13 cm) in diameter. Do not crowd the pan. Cook until large bubbles form on top, 3–4 minutes. Using a spatula, turn over the cakes carefully and continue to cook until golden on the second side, 3–4 minutes longer. Remove from the pan and keep warm while you cook the rest of the pancakes.

⚜ Divide the pancakes among warmed individual plates and top with the raspberry syrup. Sprinkle with the confectioners' sugar and garnish with mint sprigs.

Serves 4

Baked French Toast with Fruit Topping

Called pain perdu, *"lost bread," in French, this recipe rescues yesterday's bread by soaking it in an egg mixture before cooking. In a departure from tradition, these directions call for baking rather than frying French toast, with delicious results.*

8 eggs
3 cups (24 fl oz/750 ml) heavy (double) cream
1 tablespoon granulated sugar
¼ teaspoon ground nutmeg
½ teaspoon vanilla extract (essence)
4 slices dense-textured white sandwich bread or brioche, each 1 inch (2.5 cm) thick
8 tablespoons (4 oz/125 g) unsalted butter

FRUIT TOPPING
2 oranges, peeled and sectioned
½ cup (2 oz/60 g) blueberries
½ cup (2 oz/60 g) raspberries
½ cup (2 oz/60 g) blackberries
8 strawberries, stems removed and halved lengthwise
1 tablespoon granulated sugar
2 tablespoons Grand Marnier or other orange-flavored liqueur

Confectioners' (icing) sugar
Fresh mint sprigs
Maple syrup, warmed

✥ In a bowl, whisk together the eggs, cream, granulated sugar, nutmeg and vanilla until well blended. Pour the mixture into a glass baking dish large enough to accommodate the bread slices in a single layer. Place the bread slices in the dish and let soak for 15 minutes. Turn over the slices, cover the dish with plastic wrap and refrigerate for at least 2 hours or for as long as overnight.

✥ Preheat an oven to 375°F (190°C) for 30 minutes.

✥ Using a spatula, carefully remove the bread from the dish and transfer to a flat plate or baking sheet. Let stand for 2 minutes to drain off the excess batter.

✥ In a large nonstick frying pan over medium heat, melt 2 tablespoons of the butter. Carefully slide a bread slice off the plate or sheet into the pan and cook until light golden brown on the underside, about 4 minutes. Turn over the slice and cook until lightly browned on the second side, about 2 minutes longer. Transfer the slice to a clean baking sheet. Repeat with the remaining butter and bread slices.

✥ Place the toast in the oven and bake until cooked through, about 15 minutes. The toast will puff up during baking. To check for doneness, cut into the center of a piece. If it is still somewhat runny, cook for an additional 5 minutes.

✥ While the toasts are baking, make the fruit topping: In a bowl, combine the orange segments, blueberries, raspberries, blackberries, strawberries, granulated sugar and liqueur. Toss gently.

✥ Transfer the toasts to warmed individual plates. Sift confectioners' sugar over the tops. Spoon equal amounts of the topping onto each plate. Garnish with the mint sprigs and serve with maple syrup.

Serves 4

Beignets with Honey

These yeast-risen doughnuts are pure glory, and are simple to prepare.
A breakfast specialty of New Orleans, they hint of the French influence on the cuisine of the area.
Make these to take yourself back to romantic mornings spent at a French Quarter inn.

3¼ cups (16 oz/500 g) all-purpose (plain) flour, plus flour for kneading

2½ tablespoons granulated sugar

1 teaspoon ground nutmeg

⅔ teaspoon salt

1¼ cups (10 fl oz/310 ml) luke-warm milk (105°F/41°C)

2½ teaspoons active dry yeast

3 tablespoons unsalted butter, melted

1 whole egg, plus 1 egg yolk
Vegetable oil for deep-frying

½ cup (6 oz/185 g) honey, plus warmed honey for serving
Confectioners' (icing) sugar

⚜ In a bowl, stir together the flour, granulated sugar, nutmeg and salt. In a small bowl, combine the milk and yeast and let stand until foamy, about 5 minutes.

⚜ To the yeast mixture, add the melted butter, whole egg and egg yolk and whisk together just until blended. Then add the yeast mixture to the flour mixture and stir together to form a dough. Transfer the dough to a floured work surface and knead until soft and tender, about 10 minutes. Form into a smooth ball.

⚜ Lightly grease a large bowl and place the dough in it. Cover the bowl with a kitchen towel and let the dough rise in a draft-free spot until doubled in bulk, about 40 minutes.

⚜ Turn out the dough onto a well-floured work surface, punch it down, then cover with the bowl and let stand for about 15 minutes. Roll out the dough about ⅜ inch (1 cm) thick. Using a round cutter 2½ inches (6 cm) in diameter, cut out as many pieces as possible. Gather together the scraps, roll out one more time and cut out more rounds. Cover the rounds with a kitchen towel and let rise until nearly doubled in size and very light, about 20 minutes.

⚜ In a deep-fat fryer or large, heavy saucepan over medium-high heat, pour the vegetable oil to a depth of about 3 inches (7.5 cm). Heat until it registers 350°F (180°C) on a deep-fat frying thermometer, or until a small piece of dough dropped into the oil browns in about 2½ minutes. Working in batches of 4 or 5, add the beignets and fry until a nice golden brown on the first side, 2–3 minutes. Turn them carefully and fry on the second side until golden, 2–3 minutes longer. Using a slotted spoon, transfer to a paper towel–lined plate to drain. Keep warm until all the beignets are cooked.

⚜ Meanwhile, in a small saucepan over medium heat, warm the ½ cup (6 oz/185 g) honey until it is lique-fied. When the beignets are ready, lightly brush the tops with the honey and arrange them on a platter. Sift confectioners' sugar over the tops. Serve immediately with extra warmed honey on the side.

Makes 16–20 beignets

German Baked Pancake

This pancake is more akin to Yorkshire pudding than to griddle cakes, since both are based on light batters and baked at high temperatures. The pancake puffs up dramatically in the oven. Simplify the recipe by skipping the apples and serving with just a squeeze of fresh lemon juice and a dusting of confectioners' sugar.

2 Golden Delicious or other sweet apples, peeled, cored and sliced

3 tablespoons fresh lemon juice

¼ teaspoon ground cinnamon

¼ teaspoon ground nutmeg

5–6 tablespoons (1½ oz/45 g) confectioners' (icing) sugar, plus sugar for dusting

6 tablespoons (3 oz/90 g) unsalted butter

3 eggs

½ cup (4 fl oz/125 ml) milk

½ cup (2½ oz/75 g) all-purpose (plain) flour

¼ teaspoon salt

Preheat an oven to 425°F (220°C).

In a bowl, toss together the apple slices, 1½ tablespoons of the lemon juice, the cinnamon, nutmeg and 5–6 tablespoons (1½ oz/45 g) confectioners' sugar, adjusting the amount of sugar to the tartness of the apples.

Place a heavy, ovenproof 10–12-inch (25–30-cm) frying pan, preferably cast iron, over medium heat. Add 4 tablespoons (2 oz/60 g) of the butter, allow to melt and then add the apple mixture. Sauté until the apples are tender but not misshapen, 4–5 minutes. Remove from the heat.

In a separate pan over low heat, melt the remaining 2 tablespoons butter. Remove from the heat and set aside.

In a bowl, combine the eggs and milk and whisk until well blended. Sift together the flour and salt. Slowly pour the sifted ingredients into the egg mixture, whisking constantly. Add the melted butter and whisk until a smooth batter forms.

Arrange the apple slices around the bottom of the frying pan. Pour the batter evenly over the top. Immediately place in the oven and bake until quite golden and puffed up, about 20 minutes. Turn out the pancake onto a warmed platter, apple side up. Drizzle with the remaining 1½ tablespoons lemon juice and dust with the extra confectioners' sugar. Serve immediately.

Serves 2

Sun-Dried Cherry, Walnut and Sage Muffins

Among the simpler delights of country inn breakfasts are muffins, which appear with local variations from New England to the Pacific Northwest. Here, cherries and sage, two foods ubiquitous to the arid elevations of the Colorado Rockies, are imaginatively combined to satisfying effect. Good muffins, which are straight sided and slightly rounded on top, require relatively high oven heat and minimal mixing.

1¾ cups (7 oz/220 g) sifted all-purpose (plain) flour

⅓ cup (3 oz/90 g) sugar

2 teaspoons baking powder

¾ teaspoon salt

2 teaspoons finely chopped fresh sage

½ teaspoon ground cinnamon

¼ teaspoon ground nutmeg

2 eggs

¾ cup (6 fl oz/180 ml) milk

¼ cup (2 fl oz/60 ml) unsalted butter, melted

1 tablespoon finely grated orange zest

¾ cup (3 oz/90 g) pitted sun-dried cherries

½ cup (2 oz/60 g) chopped walnuts

❧ Preheat an oven to 400°F (200°C). Generously butter 12 standard-sized muffin cups.

❧ In a bowl, sift together the flour, sugar, baking powder and salt. Stir in the sage, cinnamon and nutmeg.

❧ In another bowl, whisk the eggs until blended, then whisk in the milk and melted butter.

❧ Add the egg mixture to the flour mixture and combine using only about 8 strokes. Add the orange zest, cherries and walnuts. Stir together for another 8 strokes, but do not over-mix. Some lumps are desirable, and overmixing will toughen the muffins.

❧ Immediately spoon the batter into the prepared muffin cups, filling each about two-thirds full. Bake until golden brown, 15–20 minutes. Remove from the oven and let cool for a few minutes. Serve warm.

Makes 12 muffins

Baked Eggs in Pastry with Herbs

A stylish variation on shirred eggs, this dish can be put together in steps for ease of preparation.
The pastry dough can be made up to a week in advance and stored in the refrigerator. The pans can
be lined with the pastry the night before, allowing for a speedy final assembly in the morning.

Savory pastry dough *(recipe on page 12)*

¼ cup (1 oz/30 g) shredded provolone, Muenster or similar semisoft medium-aged cheese

2 teaspoons mixed chopped fresh herbs such as tarragon, chives, chervil, thyme and/or flat-leaf (Italian) parsley, in any combination

8 eggs

2 tablespoons unsalted butter, cut into bits

4 tablespoons (2 fl oz/60 ml) heavy (double) cream

⚜ Prepare the pastry dough as directed and refrigerate for 1 hour.

⚜ Preheat an oven to 400°F (200°C). Butter and flour four 4-inch (10-cm) tart pans or ramekins.

⚜ Transfer the dough to a floured work surface and dust with flour as well. Roll out ⅛ inch (3 mm) thick and cut out 4 rounds each about 6 inches (15 cm) in diameter. Carefully transfer them to the prepared pans, pressing gently against the bottom and sides. Trim off the overhang and, using your thumb and forefinger, crimp the edges attractively. Score the bottoms and sides several times with the tines of a fork. Line with waxed paper and fill with pie weights or beans.

⚜ Bake until very light brown, 8–10 minutes. Transfer to a wire rack to cool, then remove the weights or beans and the waxed paper. Reduce the oven temperature to 350°F (180°C).

⚜ Sprinkle about 1 teaspoon of the cheese into the bottom of each cooled pastry shell. In a small dish, stir together the remaining cheese and the herbs. Break 2 eggs into each pastry shell, positioning them side by side, and dot the tops with the butter, dividing it equally. Sprinkle the cheese-herb mixture evenly over the tops, then spoon 1 tablespoon of cream atop each pair of eggs.

⚜ Bake until the eggs have set, about 8 minutes. Remove from the oven and let cool for 1 minute. Using a narrow spatula, carefully transfer to warmed individual plates and serve immediately.

Serves 4

Eggs Benedict with Virginia Ham and Corn Bread

Nothing says "special breakfast" like eggs Benedict. Here, the classic is given a southern treatment, with paper-thin slices of Virginia ham and a velvety hollandaise spooned atop rounds of freshly baked corn bread. For best results, use only the freshest eggs for poaching.

CORN BREAD
1½ cups (7½ oz/235 g) all-purpose (plain) flour
1½ cups (7½ oz/235 g) yellow cornmeal
5   tablespoons (2½ oz/75 g) sugar
1½ tablespoons baking powder
1½ teaspoons salt
⅓   cup (3 oz/90 g) vegetable shortening
⅔   cup (4 oz/125 g) corn kernels
1½ cups (12 fl oz/375 ml) buttermilk
2   eggs

HOLLANDAISE SAUCE
4   egg yolks
2   teaspoons fresh lemon juice
1   teaspoon chopped shallot
1   teaspoon white wine vinegar
1¼ teaspoons salt
1½ tablespoons water
    Pinch of cayenne pepper
1½ cups (12 fl oz/375 ml) clarified butter *(see glossary, page 124)*

2   teaspoons salt
2   tablespoons distilled white vinegar
8   eggs
6   oz (185 g) Virginia ham, thinly sliced
    Fresh chives

⌘ Preheat an oven to 350°F (180°C). Lightly oil an 8-inch (20-cm) square baking pan. Dust the bottom and sides with flour, tapping out the excess.

⌘ To make the corn bread, in a bowl, stir together the flour, cornmeal, sugar, baking powder and salt. Using a pastry blender or 2 forks, cut in the shortening until crumbly. Add the corn kernels, buttermilk and eggs and stir with a whisk until smooth. Transfer to the prepared pan.

⌘ Bake until the top is a golden brown and a toothpick inserted into the center comes out clean, 25–30 minutes. Remove from the oven, let cool briefly, then turn out onto a wire rack to cool completely. Using a round cutter 3½ inches (9 cm) in diameter, cut out 4 rounds. Slice each round in half horizontally. Set aside. Leave the oven set at 350°F (180°C).

⌘ To make the hollandaise, in a stainless-steel bowl, combine the egg yolks, lemon juice, shallot, vinegar and salt. Place over (not touching) simmering water in a pan and whisk together continuously until the mixture is a pale lemon yellow and falls in thick ribbons when the whisk is lifted, about 5 minutes. Remove from the heat and whisk in the water and cayenne. Then, while whisking continuously, slowly drizzle in the clarified butter until all of it has been used and a thick emulsion has formed. Cover and keep warm.

⌘ Pour water into a large frying pan to a depth of 3 inches (7.5 cm) and bring to a boil. Adjust the heat so the water is just below the boiling point. Add the salt and vinegar. One at a time, crack the eggs into a small ramekin or tea cup and gently lower into the water. Work as quickly as possible so that all the eggs will cook in about the same amount of time. Cook until the whites are firm but the yolks are still soft, 3–4 minutes. Using a slotted spoon, transfer the eggs to a paper towel–lined platter to drain. Trim away any straggly strands of egg.

⌘ Place 2 corn bread rounds, cut sides up, on each warmed individual plate. Top each round with an equal amount of the ham and a poached egg. Spoon the hollandaise over the top, garnish with the chives and serve immediately.

Serves 4

Classic Omelets with Fines Herbes and Tomato Concasse

Choose vine-ripened tomatoes for the best tasting concasse. For visual interest, use one red and one yellow tomato. To make fines herbes, combine finely chopped fresh thyme, chervil, tarragon, parsley and chives in equal proportions. For a moist result, preheat the pan, so that the omelet fully cooks within 60 seconds.

TOMATO CONCASSE
3 tablespoons extra-virgin olive oil
3 tablespoons finely diced shallots
2 tomatoes, seeded and finely diced, with juices
1 teaspoon salt
   Freshly ground pepper

OMELETS
12 eggs
1 teaspoon salt
   Freshly ground pepper
4 tablespoons (2 fl oz/60 ml) clarified butter *(see glossary, page 124)*, at room temperature
4 tablespoons (2 oz/60 g) cold unsalted butter, cut into small pieces
4 teaspoons fresh fines herbes

   Fresh chervil and thyme sprigs

To make the concasse, in a small nonreactive saucepan over medium heat, warm the olive oil. Add the shallots and sauté until wilted, about 45 seconds. Add the tomatoes and juices, the salt and a pinch or two of pepper. Reduce the heat slightly and cook, stirring gently from time to time, until the tomato juices have evaporated, 8–10 minutes. Remove from the heat and cover to keep warm.

To make the omelets, in a small bowl, beat the eggs until blended. Season with the salt and a pinch or two of the pepper.

Place a 7- or 8-inch (18- or 20-cm) nonstick frying pan over medium heat. When the pan is hot, add 1 tablespoon of the clarified butter, heat briefly and pour in one-fourth of the beaten eggs. Sprinkle 1 table-spoon of the butter pieces and 1 tea-spoon of the fines herbes over the surface. Allow the eggs to cook for 10 seconds, then, using a wooden spoon, begin to pull the eggs away from the edges of the pan toward the center so that some of the uncooked egg runs underneath. Cook until the eggs are still somewhat moist on the surface, but set and lightly browned on the bottom, 40–60 seconds. Using a small spatula, fold the omelet in half and gently slide it out of the pan onto a warmed individual plate. Repeat the process, wiping out the pan with a paper towel before cooking each omelet and cooking 4 omelets in all.

Spoon some of the warm tomato concasse over each omelet and garnish with chervil and thyme sprigs. Serve immediately.

Serves 4

Eggs Scrambled with Tortillas, Beans and Salsa

Favored at inns throughout the American Southwest, this preparation, known as migas, *contains the robust flavors common to Mexican cooking. Accompany the eggs with a chilled glass of freshly squeezed orange juice, infusing it with prickly pear juice for a genuine taste of the region's charming inns. All of the ingredients can be easily obtained at Latin food markets.*

1   fresh poblano chili pepper

3   corn tortillas, each 6 inches (15 cm) in diameter

6   tablespoons (3 fl oz/90 ml) corn oil

1   cup (8 oz/250 g) refried beans

8   flour tortillas, each 8 inches (20 cm) in diameter

½   cup (2 oz/60 g) chopped white onion

1   fresh jalapeño chili pepper, seeded and finely diced

2   teaspoons chopped fresh cilantro (fresh coriander), plus sprigs for garnish

8   eggs, beaten

¾   teaspoon salt

1   cup (4 oz/120 g) shredded Monterey Jack cheese

     Fresh cilantro sprigs

1   cup (8 fl oz/250 ml) bottled salsa

⚜ Preheat a broiler (griller). Place the poblano chili on a pan and place under the broiler. Broil (grill), turning as necessary, until charred on all sides. Remove from the broiler and let cool for 5 minutes, then remove the charred skin by peeling it away while holding the chili under cold running water. Cut into small strips.

⚜ Stack the corn tortillas and cut them in half. Cut the halves into narrow triangular strips. In a non-stick frying pan over medium heat, warm the corn oil. Add the tortilla pieces and sauté until slightly crisp, about 30 seconds. Using tongs or a slotted spoon, transfer to paper towels to drain. Reserve the pan and oil.

⚜ In a small saucepan over medium heat, reheat the refried beans; keep warm.

⚜ In a clean frying pan over medium heat, toast the flour tortillas until lightly browned on both sides; keep warm.

⚜ In the frying pan used for the corn tortillas over medium heat, sauté the onion in the residual oil until just tender, about 3 minutes. Add the corn tortilla strips, poblano, jalapeño and chopped cilantro. Sauté briefly, then add the beaten eggs and the salt and stir with a wooden spoon for 10 seconds. Add ½ cup (2 oz/60 g) of the cheese and continue to stir until the eggs are just set yet still tender and moist, 15–20 seconds longer.

⚜ Divide the eggs evenly among warmed individual plates. Place a spoonful of the refried beans alongside the eggs and sprinkle with the remaining ½ cup (2 oz/60 g) cheese. Garnish with the cilantro sprigs and serve with the salsa and flour tortillas.

Serves 4

Corned Beef Hash with Poached Eggs

An inspired resurrection of leftover meat, this hash derives its appeal from the tenderness of corned beef that has been slowly simmered and then moistened with some of the cooking liquid just before frying. For best results, dice all elements into ½-inch (12-mm) cubes.

1½ cups (7½ oz/235 g) peeled and diced baking potatoes *(see note above)*

5 tablespoons (2½ fl oz/75 ml) canola oil

¾ cup (4 oz/125 g) mixed diced red and green bell peppers (capsicums)

½ cup (2 oz/60 g) diced white onion

½ cup (2½ oz/75 g) diced celery

3 cups (18 oz/560 g) diced cooked corned beef

1 tablespoon chopped fresh flat-leaf (Italian) parsley

1 teaspoon chopped fresh thyme, plus sprigs for garnish

1 teaspoon freshly cracked pepper

¾ cup (6 fl oz/180 ml) corned beef cooking liquid or chicken stock *(recipe on page 13)*

2 teaspoons salt

2 tablespoons distilled white vinegar

8 eggs

✤ Bring a large saucepan three-fourths full of water to a boil. Add the potatoes and cook until tender, about 10 minutes. Drain and let cool completely.

✤ In a frying pan over medium heat, warm 2 tablespoons of the canola oil. Add the bell peppers, onion and celery and sauté until the vegetables are just tender, about 2 minutes. Remove from the heat and place in a large bowl.

✤ Add the cooled potatoes, corned beef, parsley, chopped thyme, cracked pepper and the corned beef cooking liquid or chicken stock. Toss well, cover and set aside. (The recipe can be made up to this point and refrigerated for up to 3 days.)

✤ Place a large nonstick frying pan over medium heat and add the remaining 3 tablespoons canola oil. Heat briefly, then add the corned beef mixture, spreading it out evenly in the pan. Cook until a crust begins to form on the bottom, 4–5 minutes. Using a wide spatula, turn the hash over, keeping it in one piece. Continue cooking until lightly browned,

4–5 minutes longer, reducing the heat if necessary to prevent burning. Remove from the heat, cover and keep warm while you poach the eggs.

✤ Pour water into a large frying pan to a depth of 3 inches (7.5 cm) and bring to a boil. Adjust the heat so that the water is just below the boiling point. Add the salt and vinegar. One at a time, crack the eggs into a small ramekin or teacup and gently lower into the water. Work as quickly as possible so that all the eggs will cook in about the same amount of time. Cook until the whites are firm but the yolks are still soft, 3–4 minutes. Using a slotted spatula, transfer the eggs to a paper towel–lined platter to drain. Trim away any straggly strands of egg.

✤ Divide the hash evenly among warmed individual plates and nest 2 poached eggs on top of each portion. Garnish with thyme sprigs and serve immediately.

Serves 4

Lunch

Lunchtime at a country inn is often an opportunity to dine al fresco on the terrace, poolside, or perhaps on a grand lawn in the garden. Although the surroundings will vary, the experience itself endures: gracious service of such simple midday classics as healthful salads and sandwiches puts the guest completely at ease, especially when served at an unhurried tempo.

A country inn lunch can also be just a sandwich, a bottle of mineral water and fresh fruit tucked into a pack for eating on a hike along a tree-shrouded trail. A more elaborate picnic calls for transporting hot foods in a vacuum bottle, and salads and other cool items in lightweight thermal totes.

Whether your lunch is a movable feast, a patio get-together or an elegant rendezvous on a cool winter's day, this chapter offers a variety of choices. Decorate your table with a bouquet of herb sprigs interspersed with a few garden blooms, or arrange a still life of fresh vegetables such as zucchini, red bell peppers or corn with a bit of its husk peeled back. Remember to keep your menu simple and then sit back, relax and enjoy the food, your friends and the country inn–inspired setting.

Curried Chicken Salad Sandwich

Here is a contemporary reinterpretation of the famed Waldorf salad, which was first served at the Waldorf Astoria Hotel in New York in 1896. The addition of a touch of curry powder lends this old favorite a spicy accent. These sandwiches are an ideal choice for a picnic basket.

¼ cup (1 oz/30 g) walnuts
3 skinless, boneless chicken breast halves
½ teaspoon salt
¼ teaspoon freshly ground pepper
2 tablespoons unsalted butter
⅔ cup (5 fl oz/160 ml) mayonnaise, plus mayonnaise for spreading
1 small green apple, peeled, cored and diced
¼ cup (1½ oz/45 g) diced celery
2 teaspoons fresh lemon juice
1½ teaspoons curry powder
8 slices coarse country-style bread
1½ cups (1½ oz/45 g) lightly packed mixed baby lettuces

❧ Preheat an oven to 350°F (180°C). Spread the walnuts on a small baking sheet and toast until lightly golden and fragrant, about 5 minutes. Remove from the oven and set aside.

❧ Season the chicken breasts with the salt and pepper. In a frying pan over high heat, melt the butter. Add the chicken breasts and sauté until golden brown on the first side, about 4 minutes. Lower the heat slightly and turn the breasts. Cook until golden on the second side, about 4 minutes longer. To test for doneness, cut into the thickest part of a breast; the juices should run clear and the meat should be opaque throughout. Transfer to a plate to cool completely. Cut the breasts into medium dice and place in a bowl with any accumulated juices.

❧ Add the ⅔ cup (5 fl oz/160 ml) mayonnaise, the apple, celery, walnuts, lemon juice and curry powder. Stir to mix well. Cover and refrigerate until completely chilled, about 2 hours.

❧ To make the sandwiches, lightly toast the bread slices, if desired. Spread each slice with some of the extra mayonnaise. Divide the chicken mixture evenly among 4 of the slices. Top each portion of salad with an equal amount of the lettuces and one of the remaining 4 bread slices, mayonnaise side down. Cut each sandwich in half and serve on individual plates.

Serves 4

Grilled Vegetable Focaccia with Rosemary Oil

Combining the taste and texture of Italy's famed rustic flat bread with grilled seasonal vegetables yields a wealth of flavor from simple ingredients. The wholesome sandwich is wonderful served hot from the grill, but it is also excellent eaten cold, making it an ideal choice to be included in a patio menu.

ROSEMARY OIL
1½	cups (12 fl oz/375 ml) extra-virgin olive oil
3	cloves garlic
5	fresh rosemary sprigs

GRILLED VEGETABLES
1	red bell pepper (capsicum)
4	thin slices fennel, cut through the stem end
4	slices eggplant (aubergine), cut crosswise
1	zucchini (courgette), thinly sliced lengthwise
12	asparagus spears, tough ends removed
½	teaspoon salt
½	teaspoon freshly cracked pepper
1	teaspoon chopped fresh thyme
1	teaspoon finely chopped garlic
1	fresh portobello mushroom, brushed clean
4	slices red (Spanish) onion
4	sandwich-sized focaccias
1	tablespoon balsamic vinegar
1½	cups (1½ oz/45 g) lightly packed inner yellow frisée leaves

To make the rosemary oil, in a small saucepan over low heat, combine the oil, garlic cloves and 3 of the rosemary sprigs and heat until the oil is too hot to touch comfortably, about 5 minutes. Remove from the heat and let cool completely. Remove and discard the rosemary sprigs. Add the remaining 2 rosemary sprigs to the oil and set aside.

To prepare the grilled vegetables, prepare a fire in a charcoal grill using hardwood charcoal such as mesquite or hickory.

While the coals are still glowing red, place the bell pepper on the grill rack and grill, turning as necessary, until charred on all sides. Remove and let cool for 5 minutes, then, using your fingers or a small knife, peel off the charred skin. Cut in half lengthwise and remove the seeds and ribs. Cut each half in half again. Set aside.

Bring a saucepan three-fourths full of water to a boil. Add the fennel, boil for 1 minute and drain. In a large bowl, toss together the fennel, eggplant, zucchini, asparagus, salt, pepper, thyme and garlic. Drizzle on just enough of the rosemary oil to coat everything lightly and toss again.

Brush the mushroom and the onion slices with some of the remaining rosemary oil.

When the coals have burned down to a gray ash, place all the vegetables on the grill rack and grill until they begin to appear translucent. Turn the vegetables as needed and move them around on the grill to prevent burning. The fennel and eggplant will take 3 minutes on each side; the mushroom 2–3 minutes on each side; the asparagus and zucchini about 2 minutes on each side.

To assemble the sandwiches, split the focaccias in half horizontally. Brush the cut sides lightly with the remaining rosemary oil and place, cut sides down, over the coals to toast lightly. Place the bottoms, cut sides up, on 4 plates. Divide the grilled vegetables evenly among the focaccia bottoms. Cut the mushroom into 4 slices and place a mushroom slice and a piece of roasted pepper atop each stack of vegetables. Drizzle the balsamic vinegar evenly over the tops, then cover with equal amounts of the frisée and finally the focaccia tops.

Ser

Gazpacho

The flavors of the summer vegetable garden come together in this traditional chilled soup. Bruschetta, toasted baguette slices topped here with cucumber, carrot, bell pepper and celery, is a charming accompaniment.

6   vine-ripened tomatoes
1½   cups (7½ oz/235 g) finely diced cucumber
¾   cup (4 oz/125 g) finely diced celery
¾   cup (4 oz/125 g) finely diced green bell pepper (capsicum)
⅔   cup (3½ oz/105 g) peeled and finely diced carrot
½   cup (2½ oz/75 g) finely diced white onion
⅓   cup (½ oz/15 g) finely chopped fresh flat-leaf (Italian) parsley
1   tablespoon extra-virgin olive oil
2   teaspoons sherry wine vinegar
1   tablespoon salt
1   tablespoon chopped garlic
2   teaspoons dried oregano
1   teaspoon sugar
1   teaspoon freshly cracked pepper

Coarsely chop the tomatoes. Position a food mill fitted with the medium disk over a large bowl and pass the tomatoes through it. Alternatively, simply chop the tomatoes as fine as possible; do not use a food processor or blender, however, or the bright red color necessary for the finished soup will be lost. Add the cucumber, celery, bell pepper, carrot, onion, parsley, olive oil, vinegar, salt, garlic, oregano, sugar and cracked pepper. Stir together well. Transfer the mixture to a nonreactive container, cover and refrigerate overnight.

The next day, pass the tomato mixture through the food mill fitted with the fine disk, or press through a fine-mesh sieve using the back of a spoon. Taste and adjust the seasonings. Return the tomato mixture to the nonreactive container, cover and refrigerate once again until well chilled.

Divide the chilled gazpacho evenly among chilled individual bowls. Serve immediately.

Serves 4

Provençal Garlic Soup

Despite the prodigious amount of garlic in this recipe, the resulting soup is surprisingly mellow. Trim any green tips from the garlic cloves, as they carry the sharp flavor. In springtime, borage blossoms make a lovely garnish.

8 cups (64 fl oz/2 l) water
¾ cup (3 oz/90 g) garlic cloves
¼ cup (2 fl oz/60 ml) extra-virgin olive oil
½ cup (2 oz/60 g) sliced white onion
⅓ cup (1½ oz/45 g) sliced celery
⅓ cup (1½ oz/45 g) sliced fennel
½ cup (4 fl oz/125 ml) dry white wine
4 fresh thyme sprigs
½ teaspoon fresh rosemary leaves
1 bay leaf
5 cups (40 fl oz/1.1 l) chicken stock *(recipe on page 13)*
2¼ cups (18 fl oz/560 ml) heavy (double) cream
1 slice coarse country-style bread, preferably day old, cut up
1 tablespoon salt
1 teaspoon freshly cracked white pepper

In a large saucepan, combine the water and garlic cloves and bring to a boil over high heat. Reduce the heat to medium and simmer, uncovered, until the garlic is translucent, about 5 minutes. Drain and reserve the garlic.

Return the saucepan to medium heat and add the olive oil. Heat for 30 seconds, then add the onion, celery and fennel and sauté until just tender, 2–3 minutes. Add the garlic cloves, reduce the heat slightly and sauté, stirring frequently, for another 2 minutes. Do not allow to brown. Add the white wine and cook until reduced by half.

Add the thyme, rosemary, bay leaf, chicken stock, cream, bread, salt and pepper. Stir well, reduce the heat to low and simmer, uncovered, stirring occasionally, until reduced by one-fourth and creamy white, about 40 minutes. Remove from the heat and let cool for 10 minutes.

Working in two batches, transfer the soup to a blender and blend until smooth. Return to the saucepan.

Reheat over medium heat. Divide evenly among warmed individual bowls and serve immediately.

Serves 4–6

Pennsylvania Dutch Chicken Pot Pie

In the 17th century, German, or Deutsch speakers, settled in central Pennsylvania, where they became known as the Pennsylvania Dutch. Members of this agrarian community cooked as they lived, simply and honestly. This recipe resembles a pot-au-feu more than its pastry-encased namesake.

NOODLES

1½ cups (7½ oz/235 g) unbleached all-purpose (plain) flour, plus flour as needed

½ teaspoon salt

3 eggs

POT PIE

1 roasting chicken, about 3½ lb (1.75 kg), cut into serving pieces

1 tablespoon salt

½ teaspoon freshly ground pepper

2 tablespoons vegetable oil

1 large white onion, cut into large rough squares

4 carrots, peeled

1 large parsnip, peeled and sliced

1 small turnip, peeled and cut into chunks

3 celery stalks, trimmed and cut into 1-inch (2.5-cm) lengths

3 fresh thyme sprigs, plus sprigs for garnish

1 bay leaf

2½ qt (2.5 l) chicken stock *(recipe on page 13)*, heated

½ teaspoon saffron threads

1 tablespoon chopped fresh flat-leaf (Italian) parsley

To make the noodles, sift together the 1½ cups (7½ oz/235 g) flour and the salt into a bowl. Make a well in the center and add the eggs to the well. Using a fork, lightly beat the eggs, then gradually pull the flour into the well, mixing it with the eggs. When the mixture begins to resemble a rough dough, turn it out onto a lightly floured work surface and knead for 2 minutes. If the dough seems sticky, flour the work surface again and work a little more into the surface of the dough until it is smooth to the touch. Gather the dough into a ball and invert a bowl over it. Let stand for at least 1 hour, or for up to 2 hours.

Roll out the dough on a floured work surface to about ⅛ inch (3 mm) thick. Cut into pieces roughly 1 inch (2.5 cm) square. Lightly flour the pieces to prevent sticking and cover with a towel. Discard the trimmings.

Preheat an oven to 400°F (200°C).

To prepare the pot pie, season the chicken pieces with the salt and pepper. Heat a large, deep ovenproof cast-iron frying pan or Dutch oven over medium heat for 3 minutes. Add the vegetable oil and chicken, skin side down. Cook for 2 minutes. Using tongs, transfer the chicken to a platter. Add the onion, carrots, parsnip, turnip and celery to the pan, spreading them evenly around the bottom. Return the chicken pieces to the pan, skin sides up.

Place the pan in the oven and roast, uncovered, until the chicken is a light golden brown, about 20 minutes. Remove from the oven and drain the accumulated liquid from the pan; be careful you are not burned by the release of steam. Reduce the oven temperature to 350°F (180°C). Add the thyme, bay leaf, chicken stock and saffron to the pan. Shake the excess flour from the noodle squares and add them to the pan. Stir gently to mix in the noodles, cover and return to the oven. Bake until the chicken is cooked through and the vegetables are tender, about 35 minutes longer. Uncover and cook for 15 minutes longer. To test for doneness, cut into a thigh or other thick cut of chicken; it should be opaque throughout and the juices should run clear.

Remove from the oven and skim off any fat floating on top. Divide among warmed individual bowls. Garnish with thyme sprigs and the parsley.

Serves 4–6

Duck Liver Terrine with Apple-Mango Chutney

The term terrine *refers to the ceramic loaf-shaped pan in which this preparation is baked, as well as the preparation itself. Meat molds are quite rich, so small portions are recommended. In this recipe, the tangy sweet-sour nature of the chutney offsets some of the richness. Serve with toasted baguette slices.*

APPLE-MANGO CHUTNEY

3	tablespoons unsalted butter
3	tablespoons diced white onion
¼	cup (2 oz/60 g) firmly packed brown sugar
2	green apples, peeled, cored and cut into small wedges
1	mango, peeled, pitted and diced
¼	cup (2 fl oz/60 ml) cider vinegar
½	teaspoon mustard seeds
¼	teaspoon red pepper flakes
1	bay leaf
1	cinnamon stick, about 2 inches (5 cm) long
2	whole cloves
½	cup (4 fl oz/125 ml) apple cider

DUCK LIVER TERRINE

¾	lb (375 g) duck livers, trimmed of any connective tissue
1½	cups (12 fl oz/375 ml) milk
¼	cup (2 fl oz/60 ml) port wine
1	lb (500 g) lean pork, diced
1	lb (500 g) pork fat back, diced
2	teaspoons salt
¼	teaspoon *each* ground allspice, nutmeg, ginger and cloves
½	teaspoon *each* freshly ground pepper and dried thyme
½	cup (4 fl oz/125 ml) heavy (double) cream
2	fresh thyme sprigs
2	bay leaves

To make the chutney, in a small nonreactive saucepan over medium heat, melt the butter. Add the onion and sauté until tender, about 3 minutes. Stir in the brown sugar and sauté for 2 minutes. Add the apples, mango, vinegar, mustard seeds, pepper flakes, bay leaf, cinnamon stick and cloves. Stir well, cover and cook over medium heat until the apples have softened, 5–10 minutes.

Uncover, add the cider and cook over low heat until the juices are reduced to a somewhat syrupy consistency, 10–15 minutes. Remove from the heat and let cool completely before serving.

To make the terrine, combine the duck livers, milk and wine in a 1-qt (1-l) bowl. Cover and refrigerate overnight.

The next day, drain the livers and place in a food processor fitted with the metal blade. Process until completely smooth, about 1 minute. Transfer to a bowl.

In the food processor, combine the pork, pork fat back, salt, mixed spices, pepper and dried thyme. Add the cream and process for 45 seconds. Add the liver mixture and pulse on and off until the mixture is well combined.

Press the mixture evenly into a terrine or similar container 10 inches (25 cm) long by 3½ inches (9 cm) wide by 3½ inches (9 cm) deep. Decorate the top with the thyme sprigs and bay leaves. Cover and refrigerate for 1 hour.

Preheat an oven to 350°F (180°C).

Place the terrine in a deep baking pan and pour hot water into the pan to reach two-thirds of the way up the sides of the terrine. Bake, covered, until an instant-read thermometer inserted into the center registers 140°F (60°C), 45 minutes–1 hour. Remove from the oven and remove the terrine from the baking pan. Let cool, then refrigerate overnight.

Cut the terrine into slices and arrange on individual plates. Accompany with a spoonful of the chutney.

Serves 8–10

Blue-Crab Cakes

Blue crabs are harbingers of summertime along the lower Atlantic and the Gulf coasts of the United States. They are among the prized delicacies of these areas. Serve the cakes with a southwestern slaw of tortillas, jicama and red and yellow bell peppers (capsicums).

1½ cups (10 oz/315 g) Mexican-style *masa harina*

¾ lb (375 g) fresh-cooked lump blue-crab meat, or canned blue-crab meat

⅓ cup (3 fl oz/80 ml) mayonnaise

¼ cup (1½ oz/45 g) seeded and finely diced fresh poblano chili pepper

3 tablespoons finely chopped green (spring) onion

1½ tablespoons fresh lemon juice

2 teaspoons finely chopped fresh cilantro (fresh coriander)

1 teaspoon salt

1 teaspoon dried oregano

½ teaspoon freshly ground pepper

¼ teaspoon ground cumin

½ cup (4 fl oz/125 ml) vegetable oil

4 fresh cilantro (fresh coriander) sprigs

Preheat an oven to 350°F (180°C). Spread the *masa harina* on a baking sheet and toast until it turns a nice golden brown and it begins to smell of roasted nuts, about 12 minutes, stirring once at about the halfway point to ensure even coloring. Remove from the oven and let cool completely.

To make the crab cakes, in a bowl, combine the crab meat, mayonnaise, chili, green onion, lemon juice, cilantro, salt, oregano, ground pepper and cumin. Toss together with a spoon until well blended and the pieces of crab meat lightly adhere to one another.

Divide the crab mixture into 4 equal portions and shape each portion into a ball. Flatten each ball into a round cake 3 inches (7.5 cm) in diameter and 1 inch (2.5 cm) thick. Place the cakes on the toasted *masa harina,* and turn them to coat evenly on all sides. Using your hands, press in the *masa harina* until the cakes are evenly but lightly coated and uniformly shaped. Place on a plate, cover and refrigerate until needed, or as long as overnight.

In a large nonstick frying pan, heat the vegetable oil over medium heat for 1 minute. Slip the crab cakes into the pan and cook until the bottoms are golden brown, about 2 minutes. Using a spatula, carefully turn the crab cakes and continue to cook, reducing the heat slightly to ensure the cakes heat through but do not overbrown, until golden brown on the second side, about 3 minutes longer.

Transfer the cakes to a paper towel–lined plate to drain briefly, then place on warmed individual plates. Garnish with the cilantro sprigs. Serve immediately.

Serves 4

52

Chicken Cobb Salad

This California specialty is an instant favorite everywhere it is served. Its crisp, cool appeal derives from the crunch of hearts of romaine and from its artful arrangement of ingredients, which are then tossed at the table. For a lighter version, omit the Roquefort dressing and use a simple vinaigrette in its place.

ROQUEFORT DRESSING
5   tablespoons (3 fl oz/80 ml) buttermilk
3   tablespoons crumbled Roquefort cheese
2   tablespoons mayonnaise
2   tablespoons sour cream
1   tablespoon finely chopped fresh chives
1   teaspoon finely chopped garlic
½   teaspoon freshly ground pepper

SALAD
2   boneless, skinless chicken breast halves
2   tablespoons extra-virgin olive oil
1   teaspoon chopped fresh tarragon
⅓   teaspoon salt
¼   teaspoon freshly cracked pepper
8   slices bacon
2   hearts of romaine (cos), carefully rinsed and cut into thin ribbons
¾   cup (4 oz/125 g) diced avocado
¾   cup (4½ oz/140 g) seeded and diced tomato
6   hard-cooked eggs, peeled and diced
⅔   cup (3½ oz/105 g) crumbled Roquefort cheese

To make the Roquefort dressing, in a small bowl, whisk together the buttermilk, Roquefort cheese, mayonnaise, sour cream, chives, garlic and ground pepper until smooth.

Prepare a fire in a charcoal grill or preheat a gas grill or broiler (griller) for 20 minutes.

Brush the chicken breasts with the olive oil and season with the tarragon, salt and cracked pepper. Place the chicken breasts on the grill rack or broiler pan and cook, turning as needed, until cooked through and golden on both sides, about 10 minutes total. To test for doneness, cut into the thickest part of a breast; the juices should run clear and the meat should be opaque throughout. Remove from the heat, let cool completely and then dice into ½-inch (12-mm) pieces.

Place a frying pan over medium heat. When it is hot, add the bacon and fry, turning once, until crispy on both sides, 2–3 minutes on each side. Using tongs, transfer to paper towels to drain, then chop coarsely into ½-inch (12-mm) pieces.

To assemble the salad, place the romaine in the bottom of a large platter, mounding it neatly. On top, layer the grilled chicken, avocado, tomato, eggs, Roquefort cheese and bacon. The romaine should hardly be visible.

At the table, drizzle the Roquefort dressing over the salad and toss to coat evenly.

Serves 4

Frisée Salad with Goat Cheese and Balsamic Syrup

This light salad will remind diners of a casual lunch at a French country inn. Virtually any fresh greens can be used in place of the arugula to change the character of the dish. Use this opportunity to try the chef's trick of rehydrating greens by soaking them in warm water. It works.

1 cup (8 fl oz/250 ml) balsamic vinegar

6 cups (6 oz/185 g) lightly packed inner yellow frisée leaves, tough stems removed

½ cup (½ oz/15 g) lightly packed baby arugula (rocket) leaves

4 slices baguette, toasted

4 thick slices fresh goat cheese

¼ cup (1½ oz/45 g) cherry tomatoes, halved

¼ cup (2 fl oz/60 ml) extra-virgin olive oil

½ lemon

½ teaspoon salt

Freshly cracked pepper

1 teaspoon fresh thyme leaves

1 teaspoon chopped fresh chives

✤ In a small nonreactive saucepan over medium heat, bring the balsamic vinegar to a boil. Reduce the heat to maintain a simmer and cook until reduced by three-fourths. Remove from the heat and pour into a small ramekin. Let cool.

✤ Preheat an oven to 350°F (180°C).

✤ In a sink or basin, soak the frisée and arugula in warm water to cover generously until they become very crisp, 10–15 minutes. Remove the greens from the water, drain well, cover and refrigerate until needed.

✤ Place the baguette slices on a baking sheet and top each bread slice with a slice of goat cheese. Bake until heated through, 3–4 minutes. Remove from the oven and keep warm.

✤ In a large bowl, combine the tomatoes with the frisée and arugula. Drizzle the olive oil over the top and toss to coat the ingredients evenly. Squeeze the lemon half through a sieve onto the salad; season with the salt and a small amount of pepper. Add the thyme and chives and toss together.

✤ Arrange the greens mixture in a loose mound on individual plates, dividing it evenly. Place a warmed goat cheese toast on each salad, then drizzle the balsamic syrup around the perimeter of the greens. Serve at once.

Serves 4

Croque-Monsieur

This classic French ham-and-cheese sandwich is traditionally prepared in a sandwich toaster in the shape of a scallop shell. An ordinary frying pan makes a suitable substitute, however, as is done here. Use the same technique to make a similar sandwich, the Croque-Madame, which features chicken rather than ham.

8 slices dense-textured white sandwich bread

½ cup (4 oz/125 g) unsalted butter, at room temperature

10 oz (315 g) Gruyère cheese, thinly sliced

5 oz (155 g) cooked ham, thinly sliced

Cornichons (French-style pickles)

Dijon mustard

⚜ Lightly coat one side of each bread slice with some of the softened butter. Layer half of the Gruyère slices on the unbuttered side of 4 bread slices. Top with the ham, dividing it evenly. Then top the ham with the remaining Gruyère, again dividing it evenly. Place the remaining bread slices, buttered sides up, atop the cheese.

⚜ Place a large nonstick frying pan over medium heat. When it is hot, slip a sandwich into the pan and cook until golden brown on the bottom, 1½–2 minutes. Using a spatula, turn the sandwich over and continue to cook, reducing the heat slightly, until golden brown on the bottom and the cheese melts, about 2 minutes longer. Transfer to a warmed platter and repeat with the remaining sandwiches. If necessary, the sandwiches can be reheated for 2–3 minutes in a preheated 350°F (180°C) oven.

⚜ Serve with cornichons and Dijon mustard on the side.

Serves 4

Afternoon Tea

O ne of the nicest aspects of a visit to a country inn is the afternoon tea ritual, a custom that took hold in England by the 1850s and reached its peak at the end of the century. Today, as then, afternoon tea is a graceful event that brings people together in a calming environment designed to celebrate the day.

For an authentic afternoon tea, select one or two fine tea varieties and accompany them with milk, lemon and sugar. Set out both sweets and savories from this chapter. Add color with a decorative bowl of fresh fruits or a centerpiece of flowers.

If your taste in afternoon respites runs more to happy hours than high teas, pair these same recipes with cocktails or soft drinks for equally wonderful entertaining.

Whether serving cold drinks or hot beverages, the appeal of "afternoon tea" is that it offers an opportunity to relax with friends or family—or at an inn with fellow guests—reflecting on the day, enjoying the last moments of sunshine and planning the evening's festivities. Toward this end, all these recipes are for simple fare that is easily served buffet style, so the cook can enjoy a moment's rest, as well.

Madeleines for M. Proust

There is no greater description of the magic of taking tea than that given by Marcel Proust in Remembrance of Things Past. *In it he tastes a madeleine dipped in his cup of tea, and from this simple baptism, memories of his life flood his mind. If possible, bake the madeleines in their traditional scallop shell–shaped tin plaques, and eat them fresh.*

2   eggs, separated
½   cup (4 oz/125 g) granulated sugar
    Zest and juice of ½ lemon
½   teaspoon vanilla extract (essence)
½   cup (2 oz/60 g) cake (soft-wheat) flour
½   cup (4 oz/125 g) unsalted butter, melted and cooled
    Confectioners' (icing) sugar

❧ Preheat an oven to 350°F (180°C). Lightly butter 24 madeleine molds or 12 tartlet tins, each 2 inches (5 cm) in diameter.

❧ In a bowl, combine the egg yolks and granulated sugar. Using a heavy-duty stand mixer fitted with the whisk attachment or a handheld electric mixer, beat on high speed until pale lemon yellow and the mixture falls in thick ribbons when the beater is lifted, 6–8 minutes. Add the lemon zest and juice and the vanilla and mix briefly to combine.

❧ In a small bowl, whisk the egg whites until lightly foamy. Using a rubber spatula or whisk, fold the egg whites into the egg yolk mixture until just partially blended. Do not mix them in completely at this point.

❧ Sift the flour slowly onto the egg mixture, while folding it in with a rubber spatula. Before the last bit of flour is folded in, add the melted butter and then fold in the remaining flour until blended. Do not overmix or the madeleines will not have the correct tender crumb.

❧ Fill the prepared madeleine molds or tartlet tins three-fourths full with the batter.

❧ Note: If working in batches, be sure to keep the batter barely warm while holding it and to clean and regrease the pans between batches.

❧ Bake until lightly golden brown on top, 15–20 minutes. Remove from the oven and let cool briefly in the molds. Then, using a small spoon or icing spatula, if necessary, gently remove them one by one. Sift confectioners' sugar lightly over the tops of the madeleines and serve.

Makes 24 madeleines or 12 tartlets

Coconut Shortbread

This buttery biscuit cake of Scottish origin derives its name from its crumbly texture, which is achieved by minimal handling during the mixing of the ingredients, thereby "shortening" the development of toughening proteins in the flours. The recipe given here elaborates upon shortbread's traditional simplicity with the addition of coconut for a subtle flavor accent.

¾ cup (4 oz/125 g) all-purpose (plain) flour

¼ cup (1½ oz/45 g) rice flour

¼ teaspoon salt

¼ cup (2 oz/60 g) sugar

¼ cup (1 oz/30 g) shredded dried coconut

½ cup (4 oz/125 g) chilled unsalted butter, cut into pieces

½ teaspoon vanilla extract (essence)

½ teaspoon almond extract (essence)

♕ Preheat an oven to 350°F (180°C). Butter a baking sheet.

♕ Sift together the flours, salt and sugar into a bowl, then sift together again into another bowl. Add the coconut and butter and, using a pastry blender or 2 forks, cut them in until the mixture is crumbly. Add the vanilla and almond extracts and knead together in the bowl to form a tender dough mass. Do not overmix or the dough will toughen.

♕ Place the dough on the prepared baking sheet and shape it into a round 7–8 inches (18–20 cm) in diameter and about ½ inch (12 mm) thick. Using your fingers, pinch around the edges to create an attractive border. Using the blunt edge of a long-bladed knife, score the round into 8 equal wedges. Prick the surface lightly with the tines of a fork.

♕ Bake until a nice pale gold and slightly firm to the touch, 20–25 minutes. Remove from the oven and serve warm or at room temperature, cut into wedges.

Serves 8

Honey Walnut Tartlets

This ancient remedy for winter-afternoon malaise originated in the Engadine Valley of Switzerland and dates to that area's Roman occupation. A rich, chewy confection of walnuts, caramel and honey baked in a case of sweet dough, it is sure to brighten any tea gathering.

Sweet pastry dough *(recipe on page 12)*
1 cup (8 oz/250 g) granulated sugar
3 tablespoons water
Pinch of cream of tartar
½ cup (4 fl oz/125 ml) heavy (double) cream, heated
2 tablespoons honey
1½ cups (6 oz/185 g) walnut halves, broken into large pieces
1 egg, beaten
Confectioners' (icing) sugar

⚜ Prepare the pastry dough as directed and refrigerate for 1 hour.

⚜ Preheat an oven to 350°F (180°C). Butter and flour two 4-inch (10-cm) tart pans.

⚜ Divide the dough in half. On a lightly floured work surface, roll out half of the dough about ⅛ inch (3 mm) thick. Cut out a round about 7 inches (18 cm) in diameter and set aside. Gather up the scraps and pat together. Roll out again, cut out a round about 5 inches (13 cm) in diameter and set aside. Repeat with the remaining dough, forming 2 more rounds. Line each of the prepared pans with a 7-inch (18-cm) round. Do not trim the overhang. Place the lined pans and two 5-inch (13-cm) rounds in the refrigerator until needed.

⚜ In a 2-qt (2-l) saucepan, combine the granulated sugar, water and cream of tartar. Place over high heat and bring to a boil, stirring just until the sugar dissolves. Using a pastry brush dipped in hot water, brush down the pan sides to wash any sugar back into the mixture. Bring slowly to a boil and gently stir once. Cook the sugar mixture until it begins to boil with heavy bubbles, 4–6 minutes. Watch the pot carefully and remove from the heat as soon as the sugar begins to turn a caramel color.

⚜ Immediately add the hot cream all at once, standing back and keeping your arm and hand well clear to avoid being burned by the steam. As the bubbling begins to die down, stir just until blended, then stir in the honey.

⚜ Remove the tartlet pans from the refrigerator and place the walnut pieces in them, dividing them evenly. Pour the warm caramel sauce over the nuts just to cover. Brush the dough edges with a little of the beaten egg. Lay the 5-inch (13-cm) pastry rounds on top. Pinch to seal, then press along the edge of each mold to cut off the excess dough. Brush the tops lightly with more of the beaten egg and place the pans on a baking sheet.

⚜ Bake until the pastry turns golden brown, about 30 minutes. Remove from the oven and let cool completely. Remove the tartlets from the pans and place on serving plates. Dust with confectioners' sugar. Slice each tartlet into eighths and serve.

Serves 8

Lemon Poppy Seed Cake

Nearly any type of small cake is suitable at teatime, but lemon cakes are particular favorites because their flavors complement the fine teas typically served at country inns. This cake, as easy to prepare as it is satisfying to the appetite, pairs nicely with a steaming pot of oolong tea.

½   lb (250 g) unsalted butter, at room temperature

1½   cups (12 oz/375 g) granulated sugar

4   eggs

2   cups (8 oz/250 g) cake (soft-wheat) flour

¼   teaspoon salt

1½   tablespoons poppy seeds
     Grated zest of 2 lemons

1½   teaspoons vanilla extract (essence)
     Confectioners' (icing) sugar

Preheat an oven to 350°F (180°C). Butter and flour a 4-by-9-inch (10-by-23-cm) loaf pan.

Place the butter in a bowl and, using a heavy-duty stand mixer fitted with the paddle attachment or a hand-held electric mixer, beat on medium speed until creamy, 2–3 minutes. Gradually add the granulated sugar and continue to beat until the mixture is very pale—almost white—and has doubled in volume, 4–5 minutes. Add the eggs one at a time, beating well after each addition.

Sift together the flour and salt into a bowl, then sift together again into another bowl. Add the poppy seeds. Gradually add the sifted mixture to the butter mixture, beating until smooth. Beat in the lemon zest and vanilla. Spoon the batter into the prepared pan.

Bake until a toothpick inserted into the center comes out clean, 70–80 minutes. Remove from the oven and let cool for 10 minutes. Invert onto a rack, lift off the pan and let cool completely. Sift confectioners' sugar over the top. Cut into slices about ½ inch (12 mm) thick.

Serves 8

Currant Scones with Crème Fraîche

Of Scottish origin, these tea biscuits are richer than ordinary biscuits due to the addition of eggs and cream. Warm scones are traditionally served after the tea sandwiches, accompanied by jams and whipped Devon cream. In this case, French crème fraîche, a slightly tangy thickened cream, is used in place of the Devon. Bake the scones just prior to serving to ensure their tenderness.

⅔ cup (5 fl oz/160 ml) crème fraîche

2 tablespoons confectioners' (icing) sugar

1 cup (4 oz/125 g) cake (soft-wheat) flour

1 cup (5 oz/155 g) all-purpose (plain) flour

3 tablespoons granulated sugar, plus sugar for dusting

1¼ teaspoons cream of tartar

1 teaspoon baking soda (bicarbonate of soda)

½ teaspoon salt

¼ cup (2 oz/60 g) chilled unsalted butter, cut into pieces

1 egg, beaten

½ cup (4 fl oz/125 ml) heavy (double) cream

¼ cup (1½ oz/45 g) dried currants
Jam or jelly of choice

⚜ Preheat an oven to 400°F (200°C). Butter and flour a baking sheet.

⚜ In a bowl, lightly whisk together the crème fraîche and confectioners' sugar until soft peaks form. Cover and refrigerate until needed.

⚜ Sift together the flours, 3 tablespoons granulated sugar, cream of tartar, baking soda and salt into a bowl. Add the butter and, using a pastry blender or 2 forks, cut it into the flour mixture to form large crumbs. Add the egg, cream and currants and stir together with a wooden spoon until a soft dough forms. Do not overmix, or the dough will toughen.

⚜ Turn out the dough onto a floured work surface and knead briefly just until the dough holds together. Pat it out until it is ½–¾ inch (12 mm–2 cm) thick. Using a floured round biscuit cutter about 2½ inches (6 cm) in diameter, cut out rounds and place them about ¾ inch (2 cm) apart on the prepared baking sheet. Dust lightly with granulated sugar.

⚜ Bake until golden brown, about 12 minutes. Remove from the oven and serve immediately with the whipped crème fraîche and jam or jelly.

Makes 8–10 scones

Potato Doilies with Smoked Salmon

These choice savories are simple thin potato crisps with a delicate, see-through quality similar to fine lace doilies. For the best flavor, choose only the highest-quality smoked salmon.

1   baking potato, ½ lb (250 g), peeled, sliced and julienned
½   teaspoon salt
¼   teaspoon freshly ground pepper
½   teaspoon curry powder
½   cup (4 fl oz/125 ml) vegetable oil
2   tablespoons mayonnaise
2   tablespoons sour cream
¼   cup (2 fl oz/60 ml) buttermilk
1   teaspoon chopped fresh chives
1   teaspoon sieved hard-cooked egg yolk
1   teaspoon finely chopped red (Spanish) onion
½   lb (250 g) smoked salmon, sliced paper-thin
4   small inner yellow frisée leaves
4   tiny fresh basil leaves
    Fresh chives

Place the potato in a bowl. Add the salt, pepper and curry powder. Toss well to distribute the seasonings evenly.

In a 6-inch (15-cm) nonstick pan over medium-high heat, warm 3 tablespoons of the vegetable oil. Spread about one-fourth of the seasoned potato in the oil, using a fork to design a rough shape 4–5 inches (10–13 cm) in diameter. It is important to try to keep the julienne spread thinly so that a lacelike quality is formed. The starches present in the potato will ensure that the pieces stick together.

Cook until golden brown on the bottom, 3–4 minutes, adding 1–2 more tablespoons oil and reducing the heat as necessary to keep the edges from browning too quickly.

Note: Using too little oil will cause the potato to cook unevenly, so be generous with it. Keep in mind, however, not to add too much at the start of the cooking, before the potatoes have had time to "glue" themselves together.

Using tongs, turn the crisp over and continue to cook until golden brown on the second side, about 1½ minutes longer. Using tongs, transfer to a paper towel–lined platter to drain. Repeat to make 3 more "doilies," adding more of the vegetable oil as necessary.

In a small bowl, whisk together the mayonnaise, sour cream and buttermilk until smooth. Add the chopped chives, sieved egg yolk and red onion and stir until evenly distributed throughout.

To serve, place a doily in the center of each plate. Arrange 2 or 3 slices of the smoked salmon on top of each doily and garnish with the frisée, basil and chives. Drizzle some of the mayonnaise mixture around the perimeter. Serve immediately.

Serves 4

Shrimp Salad Finger Sandwiches

Afternoon tea traditionally begins with the arrival of small sandwiches, often gaily presented on a tiered étagère. These delicate sandwiches made with shrimp will bring the salt breeze of the Georgia Low Country to your tea.

1	cup (6 oz/185 g) fresh-cooked bay shrimp (prawns) or other tiny fresh-cooked shelled shrimp
¼	cup (1½ oz/45 g) finely diced celery
1	tablespoon finely diced green bell pepper (capsicum)
7½	tablespoons (3½ fl oz/105 ml) mayonnaise, plus mayonnaise for spreading
¼	teaspoon freshly ground black pepper
¼	teaspoon chopped fresh dill
½	teaspoon salt
12	hard-cooked egg yolks
1½	teaspoons Dijon mustard
	Pinch of cayenne pepper
8	thin slices dense-textured white sandwich bread
16–20	baby arugula (rocket) sprigs
4	thin slices dense-textured wheat bread

Place the shrimp in a bowl and add the celery, bell pepper, 4 tablespoons (2 fl oz/60 ml) of the mayonnaise, the ground pepper, dill and ¼ teaspoon of the salt. Using a rubber spatula, blend together until the ingredients are evenly distributed. Cover and refrigerate until well chilled, about 2 hours.

In a small bowl, using a rubber spatula, work the egg yolks into a paste. Add the remaining 3½ tablespoons mayonnaise and blend together thoroughly. Add the Dijon mustard, the remaining ¼ teaspoon salt and the cayenne pepper and blend evenly. Cover and chill.

To assemble the sandwiches, place 4 slices of the white bread on a work surface. Spread them very lightly with mayonnaise. Divide the chilled egg mixture among them, spreading it evenly. Top each layer of egg mixture with 4 or 5 arugula sprigs just to cover the surface. Very lightly spread the wheat bread slices with mayonnaise. Place these slices, mayonnaise side down, on top of the arugula leaves, pressing firmly but gently. Now very lightly spread the exposed surface of the wheat bread with mayonnaise, and divide the chilled shrimp mixture among them, spreading it evenly. Finally, very lightly spread the remaining 4 white bread slices with mayonnaise. Place these slices, mayonnaise side down, on top of the shrimp and press firmly but gently.

Place all of the sandwiches on a baking sheet. Dampen a light towel, wring it out well and drape it over the sandwiches. Place a flat object on the sandwiches and then place a weight of 1–2 lb (500 g–1 kg) on top. Refrigerate for at least 1 hour, or for up to 4 hours if the weight is removed after the first hour.

To serve, using a serrated knife, carefully trim away the crusts. Slice each sandwich into shapes. Serve immediately.

Makes 16 tea sandwiches; serves 4

Cucumber and Smoked Salmon Mousse Sandwiches

These petite hors d'oeuvres are quick to make and are eaten just as quickly,
so be prepared to make extras. Other fillings such as egg salad are equally tasty;
experiment with them using the same basic technique for assembly.

4   oz (125 g) smoked salmon, diced
2   tablespoons mayonnaise
2   tablespoons sour cream
1   teaspoon chopped fresh dill
¼   teaspoon freshly ground pepper
3   tablespoons heavy (double) cream, chilled
4   thin slices pumpernickel bread
6   tablespoons (3 oz/90 g) unsalted butter, melted
1   English (hothouse) cucumber
     Fresh dill sprigs

Place the smoked salmon in a food processor fitted with the metal blade or a blender and process until relatively smooth, 45–60 seconds, stopping the machine once or twice to scrape down the sides of the bowl. Add the mayonnaise and sour cream and continue to blend until the mixture is as smooth as possible, 30–45 seconds longer, adding the chopped dill and pepper during the final few seconds, again stopping the machine as necessary. Transfer to a bowl and nest it inside a larger bowl filled with ice. Cover and refrigerate.

Preheat a broiler (griller).

Place the cream in a chilled bowl and whisk until soft peaks form. Remove the salmon mixture from the refrigerator and, using a rubber spatula, gently fold in the whipped cream. Do not overfold or the mixture will be grainy and will lose its shape. It should be firm enough to hold its shape when spooned out. Nest the bowl in the ice again and refrigerate.

Using a pastry brush, lightly brush both sides of each bread slice with the melted butter. Arrange the bread slices on a baking sheet and place under the broiler. Toast, turn-ing once, until golden brown on both sides, about 30 seconds on each side. Remove from the broiler. Using a round cutter the same diameter as the cucumber, cut out 4 rounds from each bread slice.

Cut the cucumber crosswise into 48 thin slices.

To assemble the sandwiches, place the rounds of toasted bread on a work surface and put a small spot of the chilled salmon mousse on each—just enough to hold a cucumber slice in place on the bread. Now place a slice of the cucumber on each bread slice and press it gently. Spoon about 1 tablespoon of the mousse onto the center of the cucumber slice, top with another cucumber slice, then repeat the process again so that there are 3 cucumber slices sandwiching 2 layers of mousse. Repeat this for the remaining toasts.

Decorate each sandwich with a small dollop of the mousse and a dill sprig. Transfer to a platter and serve immediately.

Makes 16 pieces; serves 4

Mushroom Toasts with Greens and Pear Salad

These delicious snacks utilize the flavors of four contrasting elements, yet the mélange is surprisingly well balanced. A somewhat hearty offering for teatime, this could be enjoyed as a casual snack with cocktails or a cold beer.

SALAD
1 ripe pear
4 inner butter (Boston) lettuce
   leaves
2 cups (2 oz/60 g) lightly packed
   young, tender watercress sprigs
2 tablespoons walnut oil
2 teaspoons red wine vinegar
6 tablespoons (2 oz/60 g) crumbled
   Gorgonzola cheese or other
   good-quality blue cheese

MUSHROOM TOASTS
¾ cup (6 oz/185 g) unsalted butter
1 lb (500 g) fresh portobello or
   shiitake mushrooms, brushed
   clean and diced
1 shallot, finely diced
½ cup (4 fl oz/125 ml) dry white
   wine
2 teaspoons chopped fresh parsley
1 teaspoon chopped fresh tarragon
1 teaspoon salt, plus salt to taste
½ teaspoon freshly ground pepper,
   plus pepper to taste
   Pinch of cayenne pepper
4 slices dense-textured white
   sandwich bread

Preheat a broiler (griller).

To make the salad, halve and core the pear. Using a mandoline or a sharp knife, cut into very thin slices, then cut the slices into julienne strips. In a large bowl, combine the lettuce and watercress. Drizzle on the walnut oil, toss well, add the vinegar and toss again. Season lightly with the extra salt and pepper, and toss to mix. Add the julienned pear and the cheese, toss gently.

To make the mushroom toasts, in a large frying pan over medium heat, melt half of the butter. When the foam subsides, add the mushrooms and shallot and sauté until the juices are released, 2–3 minutes. Add the white wine and cook, stirring occasionally, for another 1–2 minutes. Add the parsley, tarragon, 1 teaspoon salt, pepper and the cayenne pepper and toss to mix. Cook, stirring occasionally, until the juices have evaporated and the mixture is dry, about 5 minutes longer.

Meanwhile, melt the remaining butter. Using a small pastry brush, lightly brush both sides of each bread slice with the melted butter. Arrange the bread slices on a baking sheet and place under the broiler. Toast, turning once, until golden brown on both sides, about 30 seconds on each side. Remove from the broiler.

Using a serrated knife, trim the crusts from the toasts. Cut each toast in half on the diagonal, and place 2 halves on each individual plate.

When the mushrooms are ready, spread the mixture evenly on the toasts.

Divide the salad among the plates. Serve while the toasts are still warm.

Serves 4

Welsh Rarebit

*It is a constant in cooking that even the simplest food is splendid when the
recipe is honest and the ingredients are select. A venerated cheese dish, Welsh rarebit is
perhaps rightly dubbed Welsh rabbit, since older French references call it* lapin gallois.
Paired here with a light salad, it makes a wonderful buffet offering.

SALAD

3   radishes, trimmed, sliced and
    lightly salted

8   small pickled onions

¾   cup (¾ oz/20 g) lightly packed
    inner yellow frisée leaves

¾   cup (¾ oz/20 g) lightly packed
    arugula (rocket) sprigs

RAREBIT

2   slices dense-textured white
    sandwich bread

2   slices dense-textured brown
    sandwich bread

1   cup (4 oz/125 g) grated good-
    quality sharp Cheddar cheese

5   tablespoons (3 fl oz/80 ml)
    dark ale

2   tablespoons chilled unsalted
    butter, cut into pieces

1   tablespoon Dijon mustard

½   teaspoon salt, plus salt to taste

¼   teaspoon freshly cracked pepper,
    plus pepper to taste
    Pinch of cayenne pepper

Preheat a broiler (griller).

To make the salad, in a small bowl, toss together the radishes, pickled onions, frisée and arugula.

To make the rarebit, place the bread slices on a baking sheet. Place under the broiler and toast, turning once, until golden brown on both sides, 30–40 seconds on each side. Remove from the broiler.

In a small saucepan over medium heat, combine the Cheddar and the dark ale. When the cheese melts, add the butter, Dijon mustard, ½ teaspoon salt, ¼ teaspoon pepper and the cayenne, and whisk together until evenly melted and combined, 1–2 minutes.

Cut each piece of toast in half on the diagonal and arrange around the edges on a flameproof platter. Pour the cheese mixture over the toasts so they are covered completely. Place the platter under the broiler and broil (grill) until the cheese bubbles and starts to scorch in places, about 2 minutes. Remove from the broiler.

Place the salad in the center of the platter and serve immediately.

Serves 4

Dinner

The dinner hour at a country inn is a time of conviviality, comfort and fine food. As with the other meals of the day, the dishes will reflect an establishment's regional bias for seasonal local produce and the talents of its kitchen.

It's easy to put together your own country inn dinner. Start with one or two of the lighter items from previous chapters, select a main dish from this chapter, and then browse through the dessert recipes to round out your menu. You may want to reduce the portion sizes if you have more than three courses; you could even serve half- or quarter-sized portions, assembling a gala tasting menu as some inn chefs like to do. For a celebratory meal, plan to serve at least two different wines.

Offer a few simple hors d'oeuvres—crudités, olives, cheeses—prior to dining, to give you time to complete any last-minute preparations. Use your nicest linens and light votive candles or other small table lanterns to give the meal a special touch. Although silver place settings, crystal stemware and fine china are lovely, they are not necessary. Remember, good food and good company in a casual setting is the heart of any special dinner.

Roast Chicken with Provençal Vegetables

This rustic dish has been emulated throughout the world with different vegetables and herbs substituted when those given here are not easily available. Serve outdoors on a balmy evening just as the sun sets and you will be transported to a French auberge set amid the fields of Provence.

2 tablespoons unsalted butter, at room temperature

1 teaspoon chopped fresh thyme, plus 5 or 6 sprigs

1½ teaspoons salt

½ teaspoon freshly ground pepper

1 roasting chicken, about 3½ lb (1.75 kg)

1 head garlic

1 teaspoon plus 4 tablespoons (2 fl oz/60 ml) extra-virgin olive oil

1 cup (5 oz/155 g) peeled and cubed eggplant (aubergine)

1 small fennel bulb, trimmed and quartered lengthwise

8 bottled marinated artichoke hearts, drained and halved lengthwise

1 small zucchini (courgette), halved lengthwise

4 boiling onions, root ends trimmed

2 small plum (Roma) tomatoes, halved lengthwise

8 black olives, cured in oil and herbs

1 cup (8 fl oz/250 ml) water

☙ Preheat an oven to 400°F (200°C).

☙ In a small bowl, combine the butter, chopped thyme, ¼ teaspoon of the salt and ¼ teaspoon of the pepper. Using a rubber spatula, blend together well. Lightly season the inside of the chicken with ¼ teaspoon of the salt. Spread the creamed butter mixture all over the outside of the chicken and place in a large roasting pan. Truss and set aside.

☙ Sprinkle the garlic with ¼ teaspoon salt and drizzle with the 1 teaspoon olive oil. Wrap in aluminum foil and place in the roasting pan with the chicken.

☙ In a bowl, toss the eggplant with ½ teaspoon salt. Let stand for 10 minutes, then drizzle with about 2 tablespoons of the olive oil. Toss well to coat completely and set aside.

☙ Bring a saucepan three-fourths full of water to a boil, add the fennel and boil for 4 minutes. Drain well and place in a large bowl. Add the artichokes, zucchini, onions, tomatoes, the remaining ¼ teaspoon salt, 2 tablespoons olive oil and ¼ teaspoon pepper, and the thyme sprigs. Toss together well. Add the eggplant and mix to coat evenly.

☙ Place the chicken in the oven and roast for 10 minutes. Remove from the oven and reduce the oven temperature to 375°F (190°C). Add the vegetables to the roasting pan, spreading them evenly around the chicken.

☙ Return the pan to the oven and roast for 30 minutes. Stir the vegetables, add the olives to the pan, and baste the chicken with some of the pan juices. Continue to roast until the vegetables are browned and tender and the juices run clear when the thickest portion of the thigh is pierced with a knife, about 10 minutes. Transfer the chicken to the platter. Unwrap the garlic and arrange it and the vegetables around the chicken.

☙ Skim off any excess fat from the roasting pan and place the pan over medium heat. Add the water and deglaze, stirring to dislodge any browned bits stuck to the bottom. Transfer the contents to a small saucepan and cook over high heat until reduced to about ½ cup (4 fl oz/125 ml), about 5 minutes. Strain through a fine-mesh sieve into a pitcher and pour over the vegetables. Carve the chicken at the table.

Serves 4

Duck and Blackberry-Port Sauce with Yams

*One of the most intriguing aspects of country inn cuisine is the innovativeness
of some preparations, such as this flavorful creation based on grilled duck breast.
Any red meat duck breast—either wild or farmed—may be used in this recipe.*

BLACKBERRY-PORT SAUCE
1   cup (4 oz/125 g) blackberries
1   cup (8 fl oz/250 ml) port wine
3   tablespoons sugar, plus sugar to
    taste
1   3-inch (7.5-cm) cinnamon stick
2   fresh thyme sprigs
¼   teaspoon red pepper flakes

YAM "PASTA"
2   long yams, 12 oz (375 g) each,
    peeled and julienned
⅔   cup (5 fl oz/160 ml) heavy
    (double) cream
¼   cup (1 oz/30 g) grated pecorino
    romano cheese
¼   cup (¾ oz/20 g) thinly sliced
    green (spring) onions
¼   teaspoon salt
⅛   teaspoon freshly cracked black
    pepper

DUCK BREASTS
4   Muscovy hen duck breast halves
2   tablespoons olive oil
½   teaspoon salt
½   teaspoon freshly cracked black
    pepper
4   fresh cilantro (fresh coriander)
    sprigs

To make the sauce, in a small saucepan over medium heat, combine the blackberries, port, sugar, cinnamon, thyme and red pepper flakes. The amount of sugar will depend on the sweetness of the berries. Bring to a boil, then reduce the heat to medium and simmer, uncovered, until the liquid is reduced by one-third and the berries are tender, about 25 minutes. Remove and discard the cinnamon stick and thyme sprigs. Transfer the contents of the pan to a blender and purée until smooth, about 35 seconds. Strain through a fine-mesh sieve into a small clean saucepan and set aside.

Prepare a fire in a charcoal grill using hardwood charcoal such as mesquite or hickory.

To make the yam "pasta," bring a large saucepan three-fourths full of water to a boil. Add the yams and cook until tender, 3–4 minutes. Drain, rinse under cold running water, and drain again.

To prepare the duck breasts, rub with the olive oil and season with the salt and pepper.

When the coals have burned down to a gray ash, place the duck breasts on the grill, skin side down. Grill, turning once, for 5–6 minutes on each side for medium-rare, or to desired doneness. Transfer to a warmed platter.

Meanwhile, reheat the blackberry-port sauce over low heat until it simmers; keep warm.

In a large frying pan over high heat, combine the yams, cream, cheese, green onions, salt and pepper. Cook, stirring occasionally, until the cream is reduced and coats the yams, 4–5 minutes.

To serve, using a sharp knife, cut the duck breasts across the grain into very thin slices. Arrange an equal number of the slices on individual plates, fanning them slightly. Divide the "pasta" among the plates and top with the sauce. Garnish each serving with a cilantro sprig and serve immediately.

Serves 4

Mustard-Crusted Trout with Lemon-Sage Sauce

This recipe calls for ruby trout, whose salmon-hued fillets are somewhat thicker than those of other varieties, but rainbow trout will work well, too. Be sure to remove the row of tiny bones from the fillets prior to cooking. The fish is delicious atop a bed of mashed potatoes.

4　ruby trout fillets with skin intact, ½ lb (250 g) each *(see note above)*

½　teaspoon salt

¼　teaspoon freshly cracked pepper

¼　cup (2 oz/60 g) Dijon mustard

2　cups (4 oz/125 g) fresh bread crumbs

2　tablespoons chopped fresh flat-leaf (Italian) parsley

2　tablespoons chopped fresh basil leaves

2　tablespoons chopped fresh chives

¼　cup (1½ oz/45 g) all-purpose (plain) flour

6　tablespoons (3 fl oz/90 ml) vegetable oil

LEMON-SAGE SAUCE

5　tablespoons (2½ oz/75 g) unsalted butter, cut into pieces

⅓　cup (1 oz/30 g) diced fresh mushrooms

3　tablespoons thinly sliced green (spring) onions

3　tablespoons seeded and diced tomato

1　tablespoon fresh lemon juice

1½　teaspoons finely chopped fresh sage

½　teaspoon salt

⅛　teaspoon freshly ground pepper

⅔　cup (5 fl oz/160 ml) chicken stock *(recipe on page 13),* heated

☙ Trim the sides of each trout fillet to remove any fins and cut a small diagonal slice from the tail end to remove any tail fin. Cut each fillet into 2 pieces by slicing on a sharp diagonal to produce rough diamond-shaped pieces, season with the salt and pepper and then brush the flesh sides only with Dijon mustard to coat heavily.

☙ In a food processor fitted with the metal blade or in a blender, combine the bread crumbs, parsley, basil, chives and flour. Process until the mixture is very fine and evenly green. Transfer to a baking sheet. Press the mustard-coated flesh side of the fillets into the mixture to coat completely.

☙ In a large nonstick frying pan over medium-high heat, warm half of the vegetable oil. Working in two batches, add the fillets, coated sides down, and cook until the bread crumbs are golden brown, about 2 minutes. Turn and cook on the skin sides until the fish is opaque throughout, about 3 minutes longer. Transfer to a warmed platter and keep warm. Repeat with the remaining vegetable oil and fillets.

☙ To make the lemon-sage sauce, heat a frying pan over high heat. When it is hot, add 2 tablespoons of the butter and the mushrooms. Sauté briefly, then add the remaining 3 tablespoons butter, the green onions, tomato, lemon juice, sage, salt, pepper and stock. Bring to a boil and cook, stirring a few times, until the stock has reduced in volume and large heavy bubbles have formed, about 1 minute.

☙ To serve, place 2 trout pieces on each warmed individual plate and spoon some of the sauce on the pieces. Serve immediately.

Serves 4

Tomato Gumbo with Sea Bass

*This slightly refined version of the American southern specialty features sea bass, a species
that is present in various forms worldwide. Gumbo is a mainstay of Creole cooking, distinguished
by the use of a browned roux and filé powder, the ground leaves of the sassafras plant.*

1   whole sea bass, about 3 lb (1.5 kg), cleaned, filleted and skinned with skeleton and head reserved

5   tablespoons (3 fl oz/80 ml) vegetable oil

½   cup (2½ oz/75 g) diced yellow onion

¼   cup (1½ oz/45 g) all-purpose (plain) flour

2   tablespoons diced spicy sausage

½   cup (2½ oz/75 g) diced green bell pepper (capsicum)

1   celery stalk, diced

3   cloves garlic, sliced

1   teaspoon salt, plus salt to taste

½   teaspoon whole peppercorns

½   teaspoon dried thyme

1   bay leaf

4   cups (1½ lb/750 g) diced plum (Roma) tomatoes

2   cups (16 fl oz/500 ml) water

2   tablespoons unsalted butter

¼   lemon, sliced

1   teaspoon chopped fresh flat-leaf (Italian) parsley, plus 4 sprigs

¼   teaspoon filé powder

Cover and refrigerate the bass fillets. Wash the reserved skeleton and head in cold water, then cut the skeleton into pieces and set aside.

To make the gumbo, in a large heavy saucepan over high heat, warm 4 tablespoons (2 fl oz/60 ml) of the vegetable oil. Add the onion, flour and sausage and sauté until the flour turns a medium-to-dark brown and exudes a slightly nutty aroma, 6–8 minutes. Add the bell pepper, celery, garlic, 1 teaspoon salt, peppercorns, thyme, bay leaf, tomatoes and water. Stir well. Add the reserved fish skeleton and head and bring to a boil. Reduce the heat to medium and skim away any scum that rises to the surface. Simmer, uncovered, for 1 hour.

During the final 10 minutes the gumbo is cooking, prepare the sea bass. Cut the fillets into 4 equal pieces and season lightly with salt. In a large frying pan over medium heat, melt the butter with the remaining 1 tablespoon oil. Add the fish pieces and sauté until lightly browned on the undersides, 4–5 minutes. Turn over the fish and cook until the fish is opaque throughout, 4–5 minutes longer, depending upon the thickness of the fillets.

Remove the gumbo from the heat. Remove and discard the skeleton and head. Strain through a fine-mesh sieve into a small saucepan, pressing hard on the solids to extract as much liquid as possible. Add the lemon slices and parsley, then stir in the filé powder.

To serve, ladle the gumbo into warmed soup bowls, place a piece of fish in each and garnish with the parsley sprigs.

Serves 4

Grilled Butterflied Leg of Lamb with Couscous

Couscous, a Moroccan staple, consists of semolina wheat formed into tiny pearls.
Traditionally it is steamed for hours in a special apparatus known as a couscousière.
Here, precooked or "ready in 5 minutes" couscous yields a similar result.

1   leg of lamb, about 8½ lb
    (4.25 kg), boned and butterflied
    (about 6½ lb/3.25 kg boned)
¼   cup (2 fl oz/60 ml) extra-virgin
    olive oil
1   tablespoon chopped garlic
2   teaspoons salt
2   teaspoons freshly cracked pepper
1½ teaspoons chopped fresh
    rosemary
    Grated zest and juice of 1 lemon

COUSCOUS
4   cups (28 oz/875 g) couscous
    (see note above)
4   cups (32 fl oz/1 l) chicken stock
    (recipe on page 13) or water
⅔   cup (4 oz/125 g) diced red bell
    pepper (capsicum)
1   teaspoon saffron threads
1   teaspoon chopped garlic
1   teaspoon salt
6   tablespoons (1 oz/30 g)
    chopped green (spring) onions
6   tablespoons (2 oz/60 g) dried
    currants
6   tablespoons (1½ oz/45 g) pine
    nuts, toasted *(see glossary, page 126)*
1   tablespoon chopped fresh mint
2   tablespoons extra-virgin olive oil

    Fresh mint sprigs

Place the lamb leg in a non-reactive dish. In a small shallow bowl, stir together the olive oil, garlic, salt, pepper, rosemary and lemon zest and juice. Drizzle the mixture over the lamb, and rub it in well. Cover and refrigerate for at least 3 hours, or for as long as overnight. About 1 hour prior to cooking, remove from the refrigerator and bring to room temperature.

Prepare a fire in a charcoal grill using hardwood charcoal such as mesquite or hickory.

Place the couscous in a heatproof bowl. In a small saucepan over high heat, combine the chicken stock or water, bell pepper, saffron, garlic and salt and bring to a boil. Pour over the couscous, stir to combine and then cover with plastic wrap. Let stand for 8 minutes. Using a fork, fluff to break the couscous into individual grains. Let rest 5 minutes longer.

Add the green onions, currants, pine nuts, mint and olive oil and toss well to combine.

When the coals have burned down to a gray ash, place the lamb on the grill rack with the outside of the leg facing down. Grill for about 10 minutes. Turn over and grill until dark brown, about 10 minutes longer for medium-rare. Transfer to a large platter and let rest for 5 minutes.

Serve the couscous at room temperature or briefly reheat in a large nonstick frying pan over high heat, tossing often, for 1–2 minutes. Thinly slice the lamb across the grain and arrange on individual plates along with a mound of the couscous. Garnish with a mint sprig and serve.

Serves 8

Braised Beef Short Ribs with Mushrooms

A braise is a worry-free technique whose long, slow simmering allows the serious cook ample time to prepare other menu components, and gives the casual cook a relaxing afternoon and a substantial one-pot meal. Serve the short ribs over some creamy polenta and pair with a hearty red wine.

2   white onions
1   leek, trimmed and well-rinsed
1   celery stalk
5   sprigs fresh flat-leaf (Italian) parsley
5   sprigs fresh thyme
2   bay leaves
2   tablespoons olive oil
4   lb (2 kg) beef short ribs
1   cup (5 oz/155 g) peeled and diced carrot
2   celery stalks, diced
1   tablespoon chopped garlic
1½ cups (12 fl oz/375 ml) dry red wine
1   cup (6 oz/185 g) peeled, seeded and diced tomato
5   cups (40 fl oz/1.1 l) beef stock
2   teaspoons salt
1   teaspoon whole peppercorns
¼   cup (2 oz/60 g) unsalted butter
1   lb (500 g) fresh mushrooms such as morel, chanterelle, or porcini, brushed clean and sliced
1   teaspoon chopped fresh flat-leaf (Italian) parsley
1   teaspoon chopped fresh thyme

⚜ Cut each onion through the stem end into quarters, leaving the quarters attached at the root end, and set aside.

⚜ To make a bouquet garni, gather together the leek, celery, parsley, thyme and bay leaves and tie securely with kitchen string; set aside.

⚜ In a large, heavy saucepan over high heat, warm the olive oil. Place enough of the short ribs in the pan to cover the entire bottom. Cook, turning once, until well browned on both sides, 2–3 minutes on each side. Transfer to a platter and repeat with the remaining ribs, transferring them to the platter as well.

⚜ Reduce the heat to medium and add the onions. Sauté to color lightly on all sides, 4–5 minutes, then transfer to the platter. Add the carrot, celery and garlic and sauté until lightly colored, about 5 minutes. Drain off any excess grease and add the red wine. When the wine boils, deglaze the pan by stirring to dislodge any browned bits from the pan bottom. Add the tomato and return the onions to the pan. Pour in the beef stock, add the bouquet garni, salt and peppercorns and return to a boil. Return the short ribs to the pan, reduce the heat to low, cover and cook until the meat falls easily from the bones, 1½–2½ hours.

⚜ While the ribs are cooking, place a large frying pan over medium heat. Add the butter and when it melts, add the mushrooms. Sauté until very tender, 4–5 minutes. Remove from the heat and set aside.

⚜ When the meat is ready, using tongs, transfer the ribs to a warmed deep platter. Transfer the onions to the platter as well, arranging them around the meat; keep warm.

⚜ Strain the cooking liquid through a fine-mesh sieve into a clean saucepan and place over medium-high heat. Skim off any oil from the surface and reduce the liquid by one-third. Add the mushrooms and any accumulated juices, the parsley and thyme and bring to a boil. Boil for 5 minutes, then pour over the ribs and serve.

Serves 4–6

Pan-Roasted Salmon on Horseradish Potatoes

In this recipe, lightly peppered salmon cutlets are served atop a bed of creamy mashed potatoes brightly flavored with fresh horseradish. The flavor combination pairs wonderfully with red wine, refuting the notion that you must have white wine with fish. Pour a Pinot Noir or red Burgundy.

1 salmon fillet with skin intact, 1½ lb (750 g)

1 teaspoon salt

1 teaspoon freshly cracked pepper

HORSERADISH POTATOES

4 large baking potatoes, about 14 oz (440 g) each

1 cup (8 fl oz/250 ml) heavy (double) cream

¼ cup (2 oz/60 g) unsalted butter

1 teaspoon salt

⅛ teaspoon ground white pepper

½ cup (4 oz/140 g) peeled and finely grated fresh horseradish root

¼ cup (2 fl oz/60 ml) vegetable oil

3 tablespoons unsalted butter

1 teaspoon finely chopped shallot

1 teaspoon chopped fresh flat-leaf (Italian) parsley, plus 4 sprigs

Juice of ½ lemon

To prepare the salmon, season it on both sides with the salt. Spread the cracked pepper on a work surface and press the flesh side of the salmon into it until all the pepper adheres. Cut the fillet into 4 equal pieces and place them on a platter. Cover with plastic wrap and refrigerate.

To make the potatoes, preheat an oven to 400°F (200°C). Prick the potatoes in several places with the tines of a fork, place them on a baking sheet in the oven and bake until tender, 40–50 minutes.

While the potatoes are baking, make the horseradish cream: In a small saucepan over medium heat, combine the cream, butter, salt and white pepper. Bring almost to a boil and remove from the heat. Stir and let cool for 10 minutes. Add the grated horseradish and transfer to a blender. Process until smooth, about 30 seconds. Pour the horseradish cream into the original saucepan and let cool completely. Strain through a fine-mesh sieve into another saucepan.

When the potatoes are done, reheat the horseradish cream over medium-low heat. Remove the potatoes from the oven, but leave the oven on. Cut the potatoes in half and scoop out the pulp into a bowl. Add the horseradish cream and, using an electric mixer, beat until completely smooth. Keep warm.

In a frying pan over high heat, warm the vegetable oil. Place the salmon pieces in the pan, flesh side down. Sauté until golden brown and almost crisp, 3–4 minutes. Carefully turn over the fish and place the pan in the oven. Roast for 4–5 minutes, transfer the fish to a warmed platter and drain the oil from the pan. Add the butter and shallot, place over medium heat and sauté for 1 minute. Return the fish to the pan, add the chopped parsley and lemon juice and heat through.

To serve, divide the potatoes among warmed individual plates, top each with a piece of fish, drizzle with some of the pan sauce and garnish with the parsley sprigs.

Serves 4

Roast Rack of Pork with Apples and Onions

In apple-growing regions everywhere, autumn is harvesttime, and cider making, a ritual as festive as it is ancient, remains an important task of the season. Here, old-fashioned unfiltered cider harmonizes with onions and roast pork for a memorable country inn repast.

1 rack of pork with 12 chops, trimmed, leaving a layer of fat about ½ inch (12 mm) thick, and bones frenched *(see glossary, page 125)*
2 garlic cloves, sliced paper-thin
1 teaspoon chopped fresh thyme
1 teaspoon salt
½ teaspoon freshly cracked pepper
½ cup (4 oz/120 g) unsalted butter
2 white onions, halved and sliced
1½ cups (12 fl oz/375 ml) unfiltered apple cider
2 tablespoons cider vinegar
1 tablespoon honey
1 3-inch (7.5-cm) cinnamon stick
1 bay leaf
3 fresh thyme sprigs
2 red apples, cored and cut into small wedges
1 tablespoon sugar
2 cups (16 fl oz/500 ml) water

Preheat an oven to 400°F (200°C).

Make a series of small incisions in the fat and flesh of the pork, and insert a slice of garlic into each slit. Sprinkle the chopped thyme, salt and pepper all over the pork, then rub the seasonings into the meat. Place in a roasting pan. Roast for 20 minutes. Reduce the oven temperature to 350°F (180°C) and continue to roast until an instant-read thermometer inserted into the center of the roast away from the bone registers 150°F (66°C), or until a chop is pale pink when cut to the center, 40–50 minutes.

While the pork is roasting, melt ¼ cup (2 oz/60 g) of the butter in a large frying pan over medium heat. Add the onion slices and sauté until slightly wilted, about 3 minutes. Add the apple cider, cider vinegar, honey, cinnamon stick, bay leaf and thyme sprigs. Bring to a boil, then reduce the heat to low and simmer until the liquid is completely reduced and the onions are golden brown, about 20 minutes.

Meanwhile, in a medium-sized frying pan over low heat, melt the remaining ¼ cup (2 oz/60 g) butter. Add the apple wedges and raise the heat to medium. Add the sugar and sauté until the apples are caramelized, about 5 minutes. Remove from the heat. When the onions are ready, remove and discard the bay leaf and thyme sprigs and combine the onions with the apples. Cover and keep warm.

When the pork rack is ready, remove from the oven and transfer to a serving platter. Skim off the fat from the pan juices and place the pan on the stove top over medium-high heat. Add the water and deglaze the pan by stirring to dislodge any browned bits stuck to the pan bottom. Pour the deglazed juices into a small saucepan and boil over high heat until reduced to about ½ cup (4 fl oz/125 ml). Pour through a fine-mesh sieve into a small bowl.

To serve, spoon the apple-onion mixture around the edges of the serving platter and pour the reduced pan juices over the pork. Carve at the table.

Serves 6

Pot-au-Feu

*Here is a classic French boiled dinner, prepared in a quantity large enough
for a big family-style meal. This slow-cooking, one-pot recipe provides both a first
and second course, making it an excellent choice for casual entertaining.*

1   beef chuck roast or beef brisket,
    3½ lb (1.75 kg)
1   lb (500 g) beef marrow bones
1   yellow onion, studded with 2
    whole cloves
1   roasting chicken, about 4 lb
    (2 kg), trussed
4   celery stalks
3   leeks, trimmed, split lengthwise
    and well rinsed
3   carrots, peeled and cut into
    3-inch (7.5-cm) lengths
2   parsnips, peeled and cut into
    3-inch (7.5-cm) lengths
1   turnip, peeled and quartered
1   tablespoon salt, plus salt for
    serving
1   teaspoon dried thyme
2   bay leaves
6   fresh flat-leaf (Italian) parsley
    sprigs
8   whole peppercorns
10 slices French bread
    Cornichons (French-style pickles)
    Dijon mustard

Place the beef and the beef bones in a 10-qt (10-l) stockpot, add water to cover and bring slowly to a boil over medium-high heat. Boil for 5 minutes, skimming off any scum from the surface. Reduce the heat to medium-low, add the onion and simmer, uncovered, for 3 hours.

Add the chicken to the pot. Add water if needed to cover the chicken, return the liquid to a boil, boil for 5 minutes and skim off any scum from the surface. Reduce the heat to low, add the celery, leeks, carrots, parsnips, turnip, salt, thyme, bay leaves, parsley and peppercorns. Simmer, uncovered, until the chicken juices run clear when it is pierced with a knife and a knife blade can be inserted into the beef without resistance, about 1½ hours.

About 20 minutes before the meats are ready, preheat an oven to 300°F (150°C). Place the bread slices on a baking sheet and place in the oven until crisped, about 10 minutes. Remove from the oven and set aside. Reduce the oven temperature to 175°F (80°C).

Using tongs, transfer the chicken and the beef to a large ovenproof platter. Using a slotted spoon, transfer the vegetables to the same platter. Cover and place in the oven. Line a large sieve with cheesecloth (muslin) and strain the broth through it into a bowl. Discard the beef bones or reserve for another use. Wipe out the stockpot and add the strained broth to it. Bring just to a boil and remove from the heat.

To serve, place the crisped bread slices in shallow soup bowls, ladle hot broth over the top and serve as a first course. For the second course, carve the beef thinly, and cut the chicken into small pieces. Serve with the vegetables, spooning a small amount of the broth over each portion. Accompany with cornichons, mustard and salt on the side.

Serves 10

Stuffed Breast of Veal

Arguably the most flavorful cut of the calf, veal breast is delicious served with haricots verts. Ask your butcher to bone the breast, reserving the bones, and to cut a pocket for holding the stuffing.

STUFFING
¼ cup (2 fl oz/60 ml) olive oil
1 large white onion, finely diced
6 cups (12 oz/375 g) fresh white bread crumbs
2 tablespoons chopped fresh flat-leaf (Italian) parsley
1 tablespoon fresh thyme leaves
¾ lb (375 g) ground (minced) pork, turkey or veal
¾ cup (6 fl oz/180 ml) heavy (double) cream
2 eggs
1½ teaspoons salt
½ teaspoon freshly ground pepper
¼ teaspoon ground nutmeg
⅛ teaspoon ground cloves

VEAL BREAST
1 veal breast, 5–6 lb (2.5–3 kg) *(see note above)*
¼ cup (2 fl oz/60 ml) olive oil
2½ cups (20 fl oz/625 ml) chicken stock *(recipe on page 13)*
½ cup (4 fl oz/125 ml) dry white wine
1 small white onion, coarsely chopped
1 small carrot, peeled and sliced
1 bay leaf
1 tablespoon chopped garlic
1½ cups (9 oz/280 g) finely chopped tomatoes
1½ teaspoons chopped fresh flat-leaf (Italian) parsley

To make the stuffing, in a large frying pan over high heat, warm the olive oil. Add the onion and sauté until tender and slightly translucent, about 2 minutes. Reduce the heat to medium and add the bread crumbs, parsley and thyme. Stir until the bread crumbs are well coated. Transfer to a large bowl and let cool. Add the ground meat, cream, eggs, salt, pepper, nutmeg and cloves and mix by hand until evenly combined.

Preheat an oven to 325°F (165°C).

To prepare the veal breast, pack the stuffing into the pocket. Secure the opening closed. Heat a large, heavy frying pan over high heat for 3 minutes, then add the olive oil. Place the stuffed veal breast in the pan and brown it for 3–4 minutes on each side. Transfer to a platter. Add the chicken stock and wine to the pan and bring to a boil, stirring to dislodge any browned bits stuck to the pan bottom.

Pour the contents of the frying pan into a roasting pan with a cover that is large enough to accommodate the veal breast. Add the onion, carrot, bay leaf, bones, garlic and tomatoes. Place the veal breast on top of the vegetables, cover, put in the oven and cook for 2 hours.

Uncover and baste the breast with the pan juices. Continue to cook, uncovered, until tender, the basting juices have formed a glaze on the veal breast and a thin-bladed knife inserted into the breast meets little resistance, about 30 minutes longer. Transfer to a large platter. Strain the contents of the pan through a fine-mesh sieve placed over a bowl. Add the parsley and keep warm.

Slice the veal breast and place 2 slices on each warmed individual plate. Spoon some of the braising sauce over the slices. Serve immediately.

Serves 6–8

Grilled Rack of Lamb with Ratatouille

A traditional Niçoise vegetable specialty, ratatouille pairs exceptionally well with lamb. It can be prepared in advance and reheated, providing ample time for the cook to attend to the rest of the dinner and to the guests. A full-bodied red wine would complement this meal.

1   rack of lamb with 8 chops, about 3 lb (1.5 kg), bones frenched *(see glossary, page 125)*
3   tablespoons extra-virgin olive oil
1   tablespoon chopped garlic
2   teaspoons coarsely chopped fresh rosemary
1¼   teaspoons salt
½   teaspoon freshly ground pepper

RATATOUILLE
½   cup (4 fl oz/125 ml) extra-virgin olive oil
2   cups (7 oz/220 g) sliced yellow onions
3   cloves garlic, thinly sliced
3   zucchini (courgettes), cut crosswise into pieces ½ inch (12 mm) thick
1   eggplant (aubergine), peeled, quartered lengthwise and sliced crosswise into pieces ½ inch (12 mm) thick
2   red bell peppers (capsicums), seeded, deribbed and cut into large pieces
2½   cups (15 oz/470 g) diced plum (Roma) tomatoes
3   fresh basil sprigs, chopped
1½   teaspoons salt
½   teaspoon freshly ground pepper
2   tablespoons chopped fresh flat-leaf (Italian) parsley

✤ Place the lamb in a shallow non-reactive container and rub all over with the olive oil, garlic, rosemary, salt and pepper. Cover and refrigerate for 3 hours, or as long as overnight.

✤ To make the ratatouille, in a large saucepan or heavy frying pan over medium heat, warm the olive oil. Add the onion slices and sauté until translucent, about 5 minutes. Add the garlic and continue to cook for 2–3 minutes longer. Add the zucchini, eggplant and bell peppers and cook, stirring, until heated through, another 5 minutes. Add the tomatoes, basil, salt and pepper and stir well. Cover, reduce the heat to low and cook until tender, about 30 minutes.

✤ Uncover the pan; the mixture should still be quite liquid. Cook until the mixture thickens, another 15–20 minutes. Remove from the heat, let cool briefly and stir in the parsley. Set aside. (At this point, the ratatouille can be covered and refrigerated for up to 3 days.)

✤ Before the ratatouille is done, prepare a fire in a charcoal grill using hardwood charcoal such as mesquite or hickory.

✤ When the coals have burned down to a gray ash, place the lamb on the grill with the convex side of the rack bones facing down. Cook for 6–8 minutes, turn over, cook for another 6–8 minutes, turn over one more time and cook for a final 2–3 minutes for medium-rare. To check doneness, cut an incision into the underside of the lamb. Transfer to a cutting board and let rest for 5 minutes in a warm spot.

✤ While the lamb is cooking, if needed, reheat the ratatouille in a saucepan over medium-high heat until heated through, 8–10 minutes.

✤ Cut the rack into 2-bone portions and serve immediately, accompanied with some of the ratatouille.

Serves 4

Dessert

Each evening, a table laden with desserts of all kinds stands just inside the doorway of most country inn dining rooms. To duplicate this bounty with your own dessert course, keep in mind a few basic guidelines. Dessert is a delightful temptation, so its presentation is important. Some desserts, like summer berry pudding, lend themselves to being individually plated with just a small garnish—a few colorful berries, an herb sprig, a spoonful of whipped cream. Others, such as English trifle, make the greatest impression when displayed in an attractive bowl as part of a buffet. Allow a few minutes to pass between dinner and dessert, perhaps adjourning to another room for your finale. Serve coffee, dessert wines or brandy and have chocolates or mints on hand for nibbling.

If you are assembling a dessert buffet, choose a variety of items and styles of presentation. Offer distinctly different textures and colors such as a custard, a cake and a tart. Use a cake stand or other riser to elevate one or two items, present another selection in a deep bowl, and yet another on a wide platter.

For a simpler conclusion, choose a single recipe, keeping in mind how it fits into the menu. In general, the lighter the dinner, the heartier the dessert can be.

Plum Tart with Toasted Almonds

This rustic creation can be varied easily by substituting other firm fruits such as apples or pears. It can also be baked without fruit, and topped before serving with softer fruits such as berries or thinly sliced peaches.

2	cups (16 fl oz/500 ml) pastry cream *(recipe on page 13)*
	Sweet pastry dough *(recipe on page 12)*
½	cup (4 oz/125 g) almond paste
¾	cup (6 oz/185 g) sugar
½	cup (4 oz/125 g) unsalted butter, at room temperature
2	whole eggs, plus 1 egg yolk
7	tablespoons (1¾ oz/50 g) cake (soft-wheat) flour
8–10	red plums, pitted and sliced
¼	cup (2½ oz/75 g) apricot jelly
3	tablespoons blanched sliced (flaked) almonds, toasted *(see glossary, page 126)*

Prepare the pastry cream and pastry dough as directed and refrigerate the dough for 1 hour.

Preheat an oven to 375°F (190°C). Butter and flour a 10-inch (25-cm) tart pan with a removable bottom.

On a lightly floured work surface, roll out the dough into a round about ⅛ inch (3 mm) thick. Carefully transfer the round to the prepared tart pan and press gently into the bottom and sides. Trim the dough even with the pan rim. Refrigerate until ready to assemble.

In a bowl, combine the almond paste and sugar. Using a heavy-duty stand mixer fitted with the paddle attachment or a handheld electric mixer, beat on medium speed until evenly blended, 1–2 minutes.

Add the butter and beat on medium speed until very light and smooth, about 6 minutes.

Add the whole eggs one at a time, beating well after each addition. Then add the egg yolk and mix until a smooth batter forms, about 30 seconds longer. Add the cake flour and beat on low speed just until incorporated, about 1 minute. Scrape down the sides of the bowl and beat for about 30 seconds longer. Add the pastry cream and beat on low speed to combine, about 1 minute.

Spoon the batter into the tart shell, spreading it evenly. Arrange the plums, cut sides down, on top of the batter, pressing the plums in slightly. Place the tart on a baking sheet. Bake until the batter has set and the pastry is golden brown, 35–45 minutes. Transfer to a rack and let cool for 5–10 minutes. Remove the pan sides and slide the tart from the pan bottom onto a serving plate.

In a small saucepan over medium heat, melt the apricot jelly. Using a pastry brush, lightly brush the warm jelly over the plums and crust. Garnish with the toasted almonds. Slice and serve warm.

Serves 8–10

Harvest Apple Pie

Perhaps no dessert says casual country cooking as well as a homemade apple pie.
Indeed, there is no more hospitable finale to a country inn feast than a wedge of this classic.

Savory pastry dough *(recipe on page 12)*

2	lb (1 kg) Golden Delicious, Gravenstein or Granny Smith apples, peeled, cored and cut into slices ⅓ inch (9 mm) thick
1¼	cups (10 oz/315 g) sugar
1½	teaspoons fresh lemon juice
1	teaspoon vanilla extract (essence)
¼	teaspoon freshly grated nutmeg
¼	teaspoon ground cinnamon
⅛	teaspoon salt
2½	tablespoons all-purpose (plain) flour
5	tablespoons (2½ oz/75 g) chilled unsalted butter, cut into pieces
1	egg
1	tablespoon water

Prepare the pastry dough as directed and refrigerate for 1 hour.

In a bowl, combine the apples, sugar, lemon juice, vanilla, nutmeg, cinnamon and salt. Toss until the apples are evenly coated. Add the flour and toss again to coat evenly. Cover and refrigerate until needed.

Preheat an oven to 375°F (190°C). Lightly butter and flour a 9-inch (23-cm) pie pan and tap out the excess flour.

On a lightly floured work surface, divide the dough into thirds. Combine two of the pieces into one and, using a heavy rolling pin, roll out into a round 12 inches (30 cm) in diameter and about ⅛ inch (3 mm) thick. Carefully transfer the round to the prepared pan and press gently into the bottom and sides.

Turn out the apple mixture in the pastry-lined pan. Dot the top with the butter pieces.

Roll out the remaining pastry into a round about 10 inches (25 cm) in diameter. In a small bowl, whisk together the egg and water until blended. Using a pastry brush, brush the edge of the bottom pastry shell with a light coating of the egg mixture. Lay the second round on top and, using scissors, trim away all but about ½ inch (12 mm) of the overhanging dough. Then crimp the top and bottom edges to form a decorative rim. Cut a small slit in the top of the pie to act as a steam vent. Brush the top lightly with the egg mixture and place the pie on a baking sheet.

Bake until the crust is a rich golden brown, 40–50 minutes. Remove from the oven, transfer to a rack and let cool slightly. Serve warm.

Serves 6–8

Summer Berry Pudding

An easy-to-prepare dessert suitable for small or large get-togethers, this English country recipe needs to be prepared a day in advance. Served along with spoonfuls of lightly whipped cream, there is not a simpler, yet more satisfying after-dinner treat. If you cannot find some of the berries suggested here, use whatever is available in the market, fresh or frozen.

3½	cups (14 oz/435 g) raspberries
1½	cups (12 oz/375 g) sugar
½	cup (4 fl oz/125 ml) water
1½	cups (6 oz/185 g) strawberries, stems removed and coarsely chopped
1	cup (4 oz/125 g) blueberries
½	cup (2 oz/60 g) blackberries
½	cup (2 oz/60 g) fresh red currants
10–12	slices dense-textured white sandwich bread, crusts removed
1	cup (8 fl oz/250 ml) heavy (double) cream

In a saucepan, combine 2 cups (8 oz/250 g) of the raspberries, ½ cup (4 oz/125 g) of the sugar and the water. Bring to a boil over medium heat, stirring to dissolve the sugar. When the mixture reaches a boil, remove from the heat and let cool for 10 minutes. Transfer to a blender and purée until smooth, 30–40 seconds. Strain through a fine-mesh sieve into a bowl, pressing hard to extract all the juice. Discard the pulp and let the syrup cool completely.

Combine the remaining 1½ cups (6 oz/185 g) raspberries, the chopped strawberries, the blueberries, blackberries, currants and the remaining 1 cup (8 oz/250 g) sugar in the same saucepan used for making the syrup. Place over high heat and cook, stirring, until the juices start to flow, 4–5 minutes. Remove from the heat and let cool completely.

Dip some of the bread slices into the cooled raspberry syrup, coating both sides. Place them on the bottom and along the sides of a 2-qt (2-l) ceramic or glass bowl, lining it completely with no gaps between the slices. Spoon about ¾ cup (6 fl oz/180 ml) of the berry mixture into the bottom of the bowl.

Dip more of the bread slices into the raspberry syrup and layer them over the berry mixture. Spoon in about one-third of the remaining berry mixture, then layer again with bread slices that have been soaked in the raspberry syrup. Repeat the layering two more times, ending with a layer of bread that covers the top completely. There should not be much, if any, of the raspberry syrup left. If some does remain, reserve it for spooning on at serving time.

Place a plate that just fits inside the bowl on top of the pudding. Weigh down the plate with a heavy can or other object. Place in the refrigerator overnight.

In a bowl, whisk the cream until soft peaks form. To serve, remove the weight and plate. Cut the pudding into wedges and serve with spoonfuls of the cream and any remaining raspberry syrup.

Serves 6–8

Chocolate Soufflé

This recipe relies upon a crème patissière *for its smooth, light texture, premium chocolate for its pervasive richness and beaten egg whites for their loft. An elegant finale to any menu, this delectable soufflé is actually quite simple to prepare.*

¾ cup (6 fl oz/180 ml) plus 2 tablespoons milk

¾ cup (6 oz/185 g) granulated sugar, plus sugar for coating ramekins

1½ tablespoons cornstarch (cornflour)

3 egg yolks

2½ oz (75 g) unsweetened baking chocolate, chopped

3½ tablespoons all-purpose (plain) flour

6 egg whites
Melted unsalted butter for coating ramekins
Confectioners' (icing) sugar

⚜ In a small saucepan over medium heat, warm the ¾ cup (6 fl oz/180 ml) milk. While the milk is heating, in a small bowl, combine the remaining 2 tablespoons milk, 3 tablespoons of the granulated sugar, the cornstarch and egg yolks and whisk until blended.

⚜ When the milk is about to boil, stir 2 tablespoons of the milk into the egg yolk mixture, then add the egg mixture all at once back into the milk and whisk thoroughly. Add the chocolate and cook, whisking constantly, until the mixture thickens, 45–60 seconds. Remove from the heat and pour into a large bowl. Press a piece of plastic wrap directly onto the surface to prevent a skin from forming and let cool. When the mixture has cooled completely, stir in the flour until blended.

⚜ Preheat an oven to 375°F (190°C).

⚜ Place the egg whites in a bowl and, using an electric mixer, beat on high speed until the whites start to thicken, about 2 minutes. Gradually add the remaining measured granulated sugar and continue to beat until the whites are stiff and glossy looking, 1–2 minutes longer.

⚜ Add one-fourth of the beaten egg whites to the chocolate mixture and, using a rubber spatula, fold them in. Add the remaining egg whites and fold in just until blended; some white streaks are acceptable. The finished mixture should be a very light, foamy batter.

⚜ Lightly brush the insides of six 10–fl oz (310-ml) soufflé ramekins with melted butter, then coat with granulated sugar.

⚜ Fill each prepared ramekin three-fourths full with the soufflé batter. Place the ramekins on a baking sheet and bake until the soufflés have risen 1–2 inches (2.5–5 cm) above the edges of the ramekins, and the tops are firm to the touch, 15–20 minutes. If baked for 15 minutes, the soufflés will be moist in the centers; if baked for 20 minutes, the result will be a more cakelike consistency.

⚜ Sift confectioners' sugar over the tops. Serve immediately.

Serves 6

Lemon Galette

A galette is a thin, crisp open-faced tart. Its virtues are simplicity and flavor. This recipe can easily be doubled, plus it can be prepared up to 24 hours in advance, making this an ideal choice for entertaining.

Sweet pastry dough *(recipe on page 12)*

5   egg yolks
6   tablespoons (3 oz/90 g) sugar
2   teaspoons cornstarch (cornflour)
⅓   cup (3 fl oz/80 ml) fresh lemon juice
1   tablespoon unsalted butter, melted
    Grated zest of 1 lemon
6   very thin lemon slices, peeled

✤ Prepare the pastry dough as directed and refrigerate for 1 hour.

✤ Preheat an oven to 400°F (200°C).

✤ On a well-floured work surface, flour the dough and then roll it out into a rough round shape about 12 inches (30 cm) in diameter and ¼ inch (6 mm) thick. Be careful not to tear the dough; any holes will allow the filling to seep through during baking. Carefully transfer the dough to a level baking sheet. Repair any holes, as needed. Fold over about ⅓ inch (9 mm) of the edges of the dough toward the center. Fold the edges again in the same way to create a border about ½ inch (12 mm) high. Using fingers and thumbs, pinch the dough all around to seal the edges and to fashion an attractive crimped border. Using the tines of a fork, lightly prick the surface of the pastry.

✤ Bake until a very pale gold, 10–12 minutes. Remove from the oven and let cool completely. Reduce the oven to 375°F (190°C).

✤ In a bowl, combine the egg yolks and sugar. Using a heavy-duty stand mixer fitted with the whip attachment or a handheld electric mixer, whip on high speed until the mixture is a pale lemon yellow and falls in thick ribbons from the whip when it is lifted, 6–8 minutes. Stop the mixer, add the cornstarch and then mix again on medium speed until blended. Add the lemon juice, melted butter and lemon zest and mix until well blended. Pour into the cooled pastry shell. Arrange the lemon slices on the surface.

✤ Bake until the edges of the dough are a rich golden brown and the lemon curd has also turned golden brown on top, about 20 minutes. Remove from the oven and let cool completely on the baking sheet before slicing and serving.

Serves 6–8

116

Strawberry Shortcake

*Golden summer afternoons and strawberries are fleeting glimpses of perfection. This
is the sort of casual yet unabashedly indulgent delight that defines the country inn experience.
Shortcake, although quick and easy to prepare, does not keep well, so serve soon after baking.*

6   cups (1½ lb/750 g) strawberries
½   cup (4 oz/125 g) sugar
3   tablespoons Grand Marnier or
    other orange-flavored liqueur

SHORTCAKE DOUGH
3   cups (15 oz/470 g) all-purpose
    (plain) flour
¼   cup (2 oz/60 g) sugar
1   tablespoon baking powder
1   teaspoon salt
1   cup (8 oz/250 g) chilled unsalted
    butter, cut into pieces
1   cup (8 fl oz/250 ml) heavy
    (double) cream

2   cups (16 fl oz/500 ml) heavy
    (double) cream

To prepare the strawberry filling, measure out 3 cups (12 oz/375 g) strawberries into a bowl and mash coarsely. Stem and slice 2 cups (8 oz/ 250 g) strawberries and add to the bowl. Add the sugar and liqueur and stir together until the sugar is relatively well dissolved, about 1 minute. Cover and refrigerate for 1 hour. Remove from the refrigerator, stir well and let stand at room temperature for about 30 minutes before assembling the shortcake.

Preheat an oven to 400°F (200°C). Generously butter two 9-inch (23-cm) cake pans.

To prepare the shortcake dough, in a large bowl, sift together the flour, sugar, baking powder and salt. Add 10 tablespoons (5 oz/155 g) of the butter and, using a pastry blender or 2 forks, cut the butter into the flour mixture until the butter is in pea-sized pieces. In a mixing bowl, whisk the 1 cup (8 fl oz/250 ml) cream until soft peaks form, 2–3 minutes. Add to the flour and butter mixture and stir to combine.

Transfer the dough to a work surface, knead for just a few seconds, then divide in half. Using your hands, flatten the halves and form them into

rough rounds 8½ inches (21.5 cm) in diameter. Transfer the dough rounds to the prepared cake pans.

Bake until golden brown, 15–20 minutes. Remove from the oven, let cool for 2 minutes, and then turn the cakes out of the pans. Spread half of the remaining butter on the top of one of the cakes and the rest of the remaining butter on the bottom of the other cake and let cool for 15 minutes.

To assemble the shortcake, in a bowl, whisk the 2 cups (16 fl oz/ 500 ml) cream until soft peaks form, 4–5 minutes. Place the shortcake that has been buttered on top on a 12-inch (30-cm) platter. Spread about one-third of the whipped cream on the shortcake. Layer with the strawberry filling, half of the remaining whipped cream, the remaining shortcake, buttered side down, and the remaining whipped cream. Garnish with the remaining 1 cup (4 oz/125 g) whole strawberries. Serve immediately.

Serves 6–8

English Trifle

This dessert belongs to an enduring family of whimsically named English dessert preparations whose origins can be traced to syllabub, a frothy wine cream concoction that dates back to the 16th century. Presented in a straight-sided glass bowl (as on page 106), it makes a festive addition to a party buffet.

Pastry cream *(recipe on page 13)*

3 tablespoons cream sherry

Lemon poppy seed cake made without poppy seeds *(recipe on page 69)* or other sponge cake

2 cups (16 fl oz/500 ml) heavy (double) cream

¼ cup (1 oz/30 g) confectioners' (icing) sugar

1 cup (4 oz/125 g) raspberries

1½ cups (6 oz/185 g) strawberries, stems removed

1 cup (10 oz/310 g) strawberry jam

¾ cup (6 fl oz/180 ml) cream sherry

1 cup (3½ oz) blanched sliced (flaked) almonds, toasted *(see glossary, page 126)*

To make the sherry custard, prepare the pastry cream as directed and add the cream sherry prior to cooling. Whisk together until thoroughly blended. Let cool as directed in the pastry cream recipe.

To make the trifle, cut the cooled lemon cake or sponge cake into slices ¼ inch (6 mm) thick and set aside.

In a bowl, combine the cream and confectioners' sugar and whisk to form soft peaks. Cover and refrigerate.

In a blender, combine the raspberries with 1 cup (4 oz/125 g) of the strawberries and blend on medium speed until smooth, 30–40 seconds.

To assemble the trifle, pour about ½ cup (4 fl oz/125 ml) of the cooled pastry cream into the bottom of a 3-qt (3-l) glass bowl. Drizzle 4–5 tablespoons (2–2½ fl oz/60–75 ml) of the berry purée over the custard.

Spread one side of the cake slices with the jam. Arrange enough of the cake slices, jam-side up, in a single layer to cover the custard, then sprinkle about 3 tablespoons of the sherry over the top. Sprinkle some of the toasted almond slices over the cake, and top with a layer of the whipped cream, spreading the cream to the edges. Starting with the pastry cream, repeat the layers in the same manner until all the ingredients are used up, ending with a layer of whipped cream.

Garnish with the remaining ½ cup (2 oz/60 g) strawberries. Cover and refrigerate for at least 2 hours before serving.

Serves 6–8

Warm Chocolate Cake

This luscious creation is powerful testimony to the enduring appeal of chocolate.
A favorite way to end a meal, this particular rendition embodies the casual approach to dining
favored at country inns everywhere and is sure to be a hit at your home, too.

18 oz (560 g) bittersweet chocolate, chopped

¾ cup (6 oz/185 g) unsalted butter, cut into pieces

4 eggs

3 tablespoons granulated sugar

½ cup (2 oz/60 g) cake (soft-wheat) flour, sifted

Confectioners' (icing) sugar

Unsweetened cocoa

Preheat an oven to 350°F (180°C). Butter a 9-inch (23-cm) round cake pan.

Place the chocolate and the butter in the top pan of a double boiler placed over (not touching) simmering water in the lower pan. Melt together, stirring occasionally, until combined, then remove the top pan from the heat.

Place the eggs and sugar together in a stainless steel bowl and place over the lower pan of simmering water. Whisk vigorously until well combined, somewhat thickened and heated, about 4 minutes. Remove from the heat. Using a heavy-duty electric stand mixer fitted with the whisk attachment or a handheld electric mixer, beat on high speed until the mixture is pale lemon yellow and falls in thick ribbons when the whisk is lifted, 5–10 minutes.

Reduce the speed to low, add the melted chocolate mixture and beat until blended. Stop to scrape down the sides of the bowl, then beat on low speed until smooth. Add the flour and beat until smooth; do not overmix. Pour the batter into the prepared cake pan and place on a baking sheet. Bake for 15 minutes.

Remove from the oven and run a thin-bladed knife around the sides of the pan to loosen the cake. Invert onto a plate, lift off the pan and invert again onto a serving platter. Sift a heavy coating of confectioners' sugar over the top, then lightly dust with the cocoa. Cut into thin slices and serve immediately.

Note: The cake can be made up to 1 day in advance and reheated in a preheated 350°F (180°C) oven for 4 minutes.

Serves 8

Glossary

The following glossary defines common ingredients and cooking techniques, as well as cooking equipment, used in most country inn kitchens.

Avocado

The avocado tree bears a pear-shaped fruit with leathery skin that conceals buttery, pale green flesh. The finest flavor and consistency belong to Hass avocados, which are small to moderate in size and have dark, rough skin.

Bell Peppers

Sweet, bell-shaped red, yellow or green peppers, also known as capsicums, can be enjoyed raw or cooked. They must have their indigestible seeds removed before use.

TO SEED A BELL PEPPER

Cut the pepper in half lengthwise and cut or pull out its stem and seeds, along with the white ribs, or veins, to which the seeds are attached.

Berries

Juicy and sweet, freshly picked berries are a popular ingredient in country inn desserts and breakfast dishes. Substitute berries frozen without syrup when fresh are not available.

Butter, Unsalted

Butter enriches many country inn dishes. Using it in its unsalted form allows for greater leeway in adjusting seasonings to taste.

TO CLARIFY BUTTER

In a small saucepan over very low heat, melt the butter. Remove from the heat and let stand briefly. Using a spoon, skim off and discard the foam from the surface. Pour off the clear yellow oil into a container. Discard the milky solids. Cover and refrigerate for 1 month or freeze for up to 2 months.

Chilies

Chilies popular in the cooking of the American Southwest and Latin America lend intriguing spice to the country inn kitchen. Much of a chili's heat resides in its seeds and the white ribs to which the seeds are attached. For milder flavor, remove both before using.

Jalapeño Fresh, fairly small (2–3 inches/5–7.5 cm long and up to 1½ inches/4 cm in diameter), thick-walled, fiery variety of chili, usually sold green, although red ripened specimens may be found. Use seeded and diced in recipes or whole as a decorative garnish.

Poblano A moderately mild, fresh green—or sometimes ripened red—chili. Large and broad in shape (up to 5 inches/13 cm long and 3 inches/7.5 cm wide) it is most commonly stuffed or cut into strips as a garnish.

TO SEED AND DICE CHILIES

Always take precautions to safeguard any sensitive parts of your skin or your eyes from the volatile, burning oils present in chilies. Wear rubber gloves, if necessary, when handling chilies, and wash your hands thoroughly afterward with warm, soapy water. Cut the chili in half lengthwise through its stem end. Using your fingers or the tip of a small knife, remove the stem from each half along with any cluster of seeds that is attached. Then, use the knife tip to cut out the white ribs, or veins.

Citrus Fruit

The fruit, juice and zest—the colorful outermost rind—of lemons, limes and oranges add flavor and color to sweet and savory country inn dishes.

TO JUICE CITRUS FRUIT

Use a handheld or electric juicer to squeeze the juice from halved citrus fruits. For clearer, pulp-free juice, or to remove seeds, pour the juice through a sieve.

TO REMOVE CITRUS ZEST

You can remove the zest with a simple tool known as a zester, drawn across the fruit's skin to cut the zest into thin strips;

with a handheld fine-holed grater; or in wide strips with a vegetable peeler or a paring knife held almost parallel to the fruit's skin.

Cream, Heavy

Also known as whipping cream, this rich dairy product has a butterfat content of at least 36 percent. For the best flavor and cooking properties, buy 100 percent natural fresh cream with a short shelf life printed on the carton; avoid long-lasting varieties that have been processed by ultraheat methods. In Britain, use double cream.

Dried Fruits

Intensely flavored and chewy, dried fruits bring a homespun charm to country inn cooking. Among the many varieties available, two in particular are used in this book:

Cherries Pitted tart red cherries, usually kiln-dried with a touch of sugar to help preserve them, have a shape and texture resembling raisins.

Currants Produced from a variety of small grapes, these resemble tiny raisins, but have a stronger, tarter flavor than their larger cousins. The latter, however, may be substituted for them in recipes.

Eggs

Eggs are sold in the United States in a range of standardized sizes. Large eggs should be used for the recipes in this book.

TO SEPARATE AN EGG

Crack the shell in half by tapping it against the side of a bowl; then break it apart with your fingers. Hold the shell halves over the bowl and gently transfer the whole yolk back and forth between them, letting the clear white drop into the bowl. Take care not to break the yolk (whites will not beat properly if they contain even a drop of yolk).

TO HARD-COOK EGGS

Put the eggs, in their shells, in a saucepan and add cold water to cover generously. Bring the water to a boil over high heat, then reduce the heat to maintain the barest simmer. Continue cooking for about 10 minutes. Remove from the heat, drain and place the pan under running cold water until the water in the pan is cool. Drain and place the eggs in the refrigerator to cool completely for at least 1 hour before use.

Flour

Fresh-from-the-oven baked goods are a matter of pride for a country inn, so having the right kinds of flours on hand is especially important.

All-Purpose The most common flour used in baking, this blend of hard and soft wheats, also known as plain flour, is widely available. Bleached flour is preferable for recipes in which more tender results are desired, while unbleached flour yields crisper results.

Cake Flour Also known as soft-wheat flour. This fine-textured bleached flour is used in cakes and other baked goods.

Rice Flour A very fine powder made from pulverized rice; used to thicken cakes and puddings as well as to make noodles and very fluffy breads.

Frenching

For an attractive presentation and greater ease of eating, the ends of the rib bones on a crown rack of lamb or other cut of meat are sometimes frenched—that is, all traces of meat, fat and connective tissue are scraped clean from them to leave 1 inch (2.5 cm) or more of neat, pure white bone.

Garlic

Many country inn cooks season savory dishes with this intensely aromatic bulb.

TO PEEL A GARLIC CLOVE

Place it on a work surface and cover it with the flat side of a large knife. Press down firmly but carefully on the side of the knife to crush the clove slightly; the skin will slip off easily.

Herbs

Fresh herbs, often picked from a garden patch just steps away from the kitchen, as well as dried herbs, are a hallmark of country inn cuisine. Some common choices include:

Basil A sweet, spicy herb used both dried and fresh.

Borage Eat the leaves and blossoms fresh. The flowers make a lovely garnish. The leaves add a cucumber taste to salads and sandwiches.

Chervil With small leaves resembling flat-leaf (Italian) parsley, this herb possesses a subtle flavor reminiscent of both parsley and anise.

Chives Long, thin, fresh green shoots of the chive plant have a mild onion flavor.

Cilantro Green, leafy herb resembling flat-leaf (Italian) parsley, with a sharp, aromatic, somewhat astringent flavor. Popular in Latin American and Asian cuisines. Also called fresh coriander and commonly referred to as Chinese parsley.

Dill Herb with fine, feathery leaves and sweet, aromatic flavor well suited to pickling brines, vegetables, seafood and light meats. Sold fresh or dried.

Fennel Fine, feathery fronds resembling dill and noted for their anise flavor.

Fines Herbes Classic French blend of fresh herbs, usually including parsley, basil, chives, dill and chervil.

Mint Refreshing herb available in many varieties, with spearmint the most common. Used fresh to flavor a variety of dishes.

Oregano Also known as wild marjoram, oregano is noted for its aromatic, spicy flavor, which intensifies with drying.

Parsley Fresh parsley is used both to flavor long-simmered dishes and as a garnish. The flat-leaf (Italian) variety has a more pronounced flavor that makes it generally preferable to the curly-leaf type.

Rosemary Used either fresh or dried, strong-flavored rosemary frequently scents meat dishes, as well as seafood and vegetables. Use it sparingly, except when grilling.

Sage Fresh or dried, this pungent herb goes well with pork, lamb, veal or poultry.

Tarragon Fresh or dried, this sweet, fragrant herb seasons salads, seafood, chicken, light meats, eggs and vegetables.

Thyme This delicately fragrant, clean-tasting, small-leaved herb is used fresh or dried to flavor poultry, lamb, seafood and vegetables.

TO STORE FRESH HERBS

Culinary herbs add great flavor and visual appeal to country inn–style dishes and can add a charming touch to a kitchen as well. Store fresh herbs in water—as you would cut flowers—awaiting use. Place different herbs in separate glass containers and align them on a countertop or shelf. Trimmed daily, with the water changed, they will keep for up to 1 week.

Leeks

These sweet, moderately flavored members of the onion family are long and cylindrical, with a pale white root end and dark green leaves.

TO CLEAN A LEEK
Grown in sandy soil, leeks tend to collect grit between their tightly layered leaves. After trimming the root and tough green ends, cut the leek completely in half lengthwise; or, if the leek is to be cooked whole, make a deep lengthwise slit starting near the root end and extending upward toward the leaves. Fill a basin or sink with cold water and swish the leek vigorously in the water to wash out the grit; drain and rinse the sink well, then refill it and repeat the procedure until no grit remains in the sink.

Masa Harina

A fine flour ground from corn kernels, *masa harina*—Spanish for "dough flour"—is used to prepare the dough for corn tortillas. Mexican-style has been soaked in slaked lime. Caribbean-style is just very finely ground corn kernels. While the results will taste different, they can be used interchangeably in recipes.

Mushrooms

With their rich, earthy flavors and meaty textures, mushrooms are frequently featured on the menus of country inns. Most varieties are available fresh and dried. Fresh mushrooms must be cleansed of dirt with a soft-bristled brush or wiped clean with a kitchen towel. They should not be rinsed with water, as the moisture ruins their texture. Dried mushrooms must be rehydrated before using.

Nutmeg

A sweet spice derived from the pit of the nutmeg tree's fruit. Sold ground or whole to be grated as needed.

Nuts

Country inn cooks make use of a wide variety of nuts in savory and sweet dishes.

Almonds Mellow, sweet, widely popular oval nuts, sometimes purchased blanched, that is, with their skins removed, and thinly sliced (flaked).

Macadamias Large, spherical nuts with a crisp texture and rich, buttery flavor. Native to Australia, macadamias are now

grown mostly in Hawaii and Central America.

Pine Nuts These small, ivory-colored nuts are the seeds of a species of pine tree and have a rich, delicately resinous flavor.

Walnuts These crinkly nuts have a rich, slightly astringent flavor and crisp texture. English walnuts are the most common variety, but American black walnuts are prized for their finer flavor.

TO TOAST NUTS
Toast nuts to bring out their full flavor and aroma. Place a single layer of nuts in a dry heavy frying pan over low heat. Toast, stirring or tossing frequently to prevent scorching, just until their color deepens.

Onions

Onions form an indispensable part of the country inn pantry.

Green Onions A variety harvested immature, with both its small white bulb and its long green leaves enjoyed raw or cooked. Also known as spring onions or scallions.

Red Onions A mild, sweet variety with purplish red skin and red-tinged white flesh. Also known as Spanish onions.

White Onions White-skinned, white-fleshed variety with a sweet and mild flavor. If unavailable, substitute mild yellow onions.

Yellow Onions The common white-fleshed, strong-flavored variety with dry, yellowish brown skins.

Ramekins

Small, heatproof containers, usually made of white porcelain, glazed earthenware or glass, used for a wide variety of individual-portion presentations, ranging from eggs to soufflés.

Shallots

These small cousins of the onion have a papery brown skin, purple-tinged flesh and a flavor resembling both sweet onion and garlic.

Syrup

Dark, rich and intensely sweet maple syrup adds special savor to breakfast; buy only products labeled "pure." Fruit syrups are also popular for topping pancakes, waffles and ice cream.

COUNTRY INN: THE BEST OF CASUAL COUNTRY COOKING

TO WARM SYRUP

Pour the syrup into a small heatproof serving pitcher and stand the pitcher in 1–2 inches (2.5–5 cm) of gently simmering water.

Tea

Afternoon tea is a ritual at many country inns. The best type of tea to serve in the afternoon is what is known as a black tea, the term for tea leaves that have been allowed to ferment fully after they are picked and before they are dried. These yield a rich, strong, dark and aromatic cup of tea that can be enjoyed plain or with lemon or milk.

Familiar black varieties include Indian Assam, which is pungent and malty; Ceylon, which is slightly softer; Darjeeling, which is a deep reddish brown, full-flavored tea from northeastern India; thick-bodied keemun from northern China; and smoky Lapsang souchong, which is produced in China, India and Indonesia. The most popular herbal teas are peppermint and chamomile and blends that include rosehips, cinnamon and other aromatic ingredients.

TO BREW TEA

Bring fresh, cold water to a full rolling boil. Preheat the teapot by pouring in about 1 inch (2.5 cm) of hot water, swirling it around and pouring it out. Put 1 rounded teaspoon of tea leaves per cup into the pot, adding 1 teaspoon extra for pots holding 6 or more cups; alternatively, put the tea into an infusion ball. Add boiling water and steep for 3 minutes before serving. If not using an infusion ball, pour the tea through a fine-mesh strainer into each cup.

Tomatoes

Tomatoes from the garden find their way into every course of a country inn meal except dessert. In summer, seek out the best vine-ripened tomatoes you can find for the finest flavor and texture. For use in salads or hors d'oeuvres, look for bite-sized cherry tomatoes. The most familiar variety of tomato to offer year-round quality is the Italian plum tomato, also known as the Roma or egg tomato.

TO SEED TOMATOES

Cut them in half crosswise and squeeze gently to force out the seed sacs.

Vinegars

The term *vinegar* refers to any alcoholic liquid caused to ferment a second time by certain strains of yeast, turning it highly acidic. When the sharp acidity of vinegar is desired without any particular character, use distilled white vinegar.

Wine Glasses

Clear glass, long stems and a rim narrower than the widest part of the bowl are requisites for the proper appreciation of a wine's color and to concentrate its bouquet. In general pour a red wine into a glass with a bowl deeper and wider than that for a white wine.

Zucchini

These slender, cylindrical, green summer squashes, also known as courgettes, often grow in abundance in country inn gardens. Seek out smaller zucchini, which have a finer texture and tinier seeds than more mature specimens. In spring, well-stocked greengrocers often sell zucchini with their delicate, edible blossoms still attached.

ACKNOWLEDGMENTS

George Mahaffey would like to thank his wife, Jamie, for her patience and support during the writing of this book as well as his children, Michael, Tristan, Rian, Reghan and Finn, without whose love for playing outdoors in the Colorado summer this book would not have been possible. He would also like to express his gratitude to both Jill Fox and Lisa Atwood for their guiding hands and tireless editorial support. Finally, a word of thanks to Norman Kolpas, whose friendship is greatly appreciated.

For lending photographic props, the photographer and stylist would especially like to thank: Fillamento, as well as American Rag Maison and Naomi's Pottery, all of San Francisco, California.

For their valuable editorial support, the publishers thank: Desne Border, Ken DellaPenta and Peggy Fallon.

Index

COUNTRY INN: THE BEST OF CASUAL COUNTRY COOKING